IMPLICATIONS OF NEW TECHNOLOGY FOR THE SCHOOL CURRICULUM

IMPLICATIONS OF NEW TECHNOLOGY FOR THE SCHOOL CURRICULUM

Richard Fothergill

KOGAN
PAGE

Dedication

To all those who worked in small and large ways in the
Microelectronics Education Programme, and gave me such
support and inspiration.

First published in 1988 by Kogan Page Ltd,
120 Pentonville Road, London N1 9JN

Typeset by DP Photosetting, Aylesbury, Bucks
Printed and bound in Great Britain by
Billings Book Plan, Worcester

British Library Cataloguing in Publication Data
Fothergill, Richard, *1937–*
   Implications of new technology for the
   school curriculum.
   1. Education. Implications of technological
   development
   I. Title
   370

ISBN 1-85091-584-9

Contents

Acknowledgements

While a number of publications are quoted in the text, these are only a small sample of the numerous books, journals, newspapers and dialogues with software that I have read and experienced in the last decade and which have formed part of the background to the thinking behind this book. Also very important are the many stimulating conversations I have had here and overseas, particularly with my many colleagues in Europe, that have made a strong impact on my ideas. Some may even recognise their words although I cannot now remember who said them. To all those sources I am indebted and grateful, even though they are not separately identified.

I am also grateful for the technical help provided by the Northern Region Information Centre, Bill Broderick and Jackie Day, and for the patience of Dolores Black at Kogan Page who, after first encouraging me to write this book, then had to wait so long for the final text.

All other responsibilities are entirely mine.

Part 1

The Background

The first school computer

In September 1965, at The Royal Liberty School, Bill Broderick was leaning back in his chair, considering the efforts of the last 18 months that were reaching their fruition that day. The Elliot 920A computer was being delivered – a temporary installation until the next model, the 903, would be ready the following year. Exhilaration was the dominant feeling, but there was also an immense sense of relief that all the hard work had succeeded and great anticipation that the courses that had been planned and dreamed about would actually begin to take place.

It appears that The Royal Liberty in Romford was the first school to purchase a computer. Bill had been interested in the idea of using computer programming as an aid to understanding maths since his days on PGCE at Hull University in 1961, further stimulated by discussions with the assistant personnel manager at ICL (then ICT). His conviction was that

> ... learning to program a computer was an educational exercise, apart from its vocational value; before he can program a problem the student has first to understand it fully, while the actual programming gives him valuable practice in clear and logical thinking. (Broderick, 1968)

Theoretical programming is possible and became fashionable in many schools in later years, but having an actual computer present in the school – its own property – gave a continuing sense of reality to the work. For many schools at that time (as for the next 15 years) this was an impossible dream, as funds for such a purchase would not be available. The common solution was the circulation of a terminal to the mainframe used by the local authority. The computer would arrive at the school for its annual three-week stay (the time varied between schools and authorities) and the children would rush to type in their year's creations, waiting expectantly for print-outs that showed they had worked. Others used the local university, polytechnic or, occasionally, well-equipped college, but the same restrictions of time and accessibility marred the work for there was no sense of continuity and opportunity for developing the program.

At The Royal Liberty, they were getting their *own* machine. It had not been easy; rather it had come from a young man's determination and persistence to prove that his dream could be made a reality. Back in 1963 he had convinced the headmaster that it was a worthy target, but of course there was no money. £15,000 was worth much more then than it is now, and was thus a substantial sum for a school to find. Out into the world of commerce and industry went letters appealing for donations and support, and back came mainly silence, occasional refusals and, very rarely, a few tens of pounds. This was the time of local government reorganisation, and the local authority, a district of Essex, was about to become part of a Metropolitan Borough of Greater London. What better start for an education committee than to provide some money for such a prestigious and innovative purchase! So they promised, but the amount was only a third of what was needed.

In the Autumn of 1964 an enthusiastic parent offered his services as a fund-raiser. He was a man of energy and experience, and the vigour of the appeal for funds took on a new dimension. Advertisements were placed in the *Financial Times* and elsewhere, and the money began to appear. By May 1965, enough funds had been accumulated to justify an order to Elliot Automation. The London Borough of Havering and The Royal Liberty School had purchased a computer – now it was arriving!

The plan was to aim for a GCE A-level course in Computer Science, but the University of London did not offer such an exam. As it would take two years to develop, an alternative was necessary and the syllabus finally adopted omitted all reference to the technology and appeared more like computer-oriented mathematics, which was compatible with the A-level Pure Mathematics course.

Thus began one of the first significant adventures with a computer in a school. There had been difficulties in persuading people that it was a sensible idea, in finding the money, and in locating timetable space and an appropriate syllabus that coincided with the thinking of an examination board. Such problems dog most educational innovations, and continue to be an issue for computing for many years, but they are usually overcome or at least reduced by a persistent and determined teacher charged with an important and appropriate idea. Such was the case at The Royal Liberty School.

Discovering

During this period I was teaching in the biology laboratory at South West Ham Technical School. Large windows surrounded it on three of the four sides. Showing films required the use of expensive blackout, and it was difficult to avoid reflections on most types of screen. but biology was proving a popular subject. This was in spite of a relentlessly factual syllabus, which for the less able children had to be given extra excitement in order to provide interest. Far too much time was spent on remembering names, reciting notes and recalling diagrams, but this was the way to pass examinations and these were and still are the signs of success that the children needed.

During the summer, however, a new and apparently exciting light had appeared for some of us. I was much involved in some in-service training of the new Nuffield Biology scheme. Later, with the help of colleagues, I used my laboratory for week-long courses to introduce the potential of this new approach to teachers from three London boroughs, including Havering. Indeed, although we were never given the title, we took on many of the roles of 'advisory teachers' to support the beginning of this new venture.

Each local education authority was providing some money to help schools to invest in the equipment necessary to start the course, but like all such funding it was not enough. Substantial investment in books, equipment, apparatus and materials was needed to adapt our basically theoretical teaching to the much more practical orientation of the Nuffield scheme. Teaching biology had always included much practical work, but was more inclined to the 'set piece' than the exploratory activity that the new approach required. Some of the apparatus was expensive and was only used occasionally during the course; the teacher at a school nearby agreed to share one major item with me, so that between us only one food calorimeter was purchased. While causing some administrative anxieties, this proved a perfectly practical answer to the financial problem.

The Nuffield approach caught our imagination strongly. By handing much of the learning over to the children, it enabled them to explore and discover their understanding rather than being constantly told of it. Of course, this was a much slower approach; it caused some criticism as it meant that less territory was covered in each syllabus, but for those of us involved, it appeared to help the children to create the learning and understanding that had been missing in previous syllabuses. The emphasis on practical work was much more stimulating for us and it certainly appeared to be more motivating for the children. However, it was also more challenging to their thinking, and success was no longer so dependent on a good memory. For some children this was not such a good idea.

The aims of the course seemed quite revolutionary at the time, as in the main they were so general. They were:

    a. to develop and encourage an attitude of curiosity and enquiry;
    b. to develop a comtemporary outlook on the subject;

    c. to develop an understanding of man as a living organism and his place in nature;

    d. to foster a realisation of the variety of life and of underlying similarities among living things;

    e. to encourage a respect and feeling for all living things;

    f. to teach the art of planning scientific investigations, the formulation of questions, and the design of experiments;

    g. to develop a critical approach to evidence;

    h. to develop the following ideas about biology as part of human endeavour:

        1. that biology has been developing over many centuries; there are many unanswered questions about life; our ideas of life may change as new knowledge is obtained;

        2. that biological knowledge is the product of scientists working in many different parts of the world. Its pursuit is international;

        3. that it is based not only on observation and experimentation but also on questioning, the formulation of hypotheses, testing of hypotheses and, above all, on communication between people;

        4. that developments in chemistry, physics, and mathematics are helping us to make advances in biology. (Nuffield, 1966)

Teaching towards such aims led to much more interest in the attitudes of the children and much less to the factual content. By exploring to find out answers and trends, the children developed a respect for accuracy rather than the 'right answer', as frequently (particularly when faced with the large amount of variation in living things) there was no such thing as the 'right result' – only the 'child's result'. Of course, there were many occasions when the children did the work wrongly, but this was as important a learning occasion as when they did it right. Most of the practical work was conducted in groups and led to heated debates between the children.

For the teachers on the in-service courses, and later when they took their own classes in school, the real difficulties related to their own position and role. For some the change was going to be too much for them to accept, while for others the school atmosphere was too intimidating for them to persist. If the school's idea of order and good behaviour was a silent or regimented classroom (and it frequently was in the 1960s), the highly practical and talkative work that brought the best out of the Nuffield approach created problems. Traditional approaches never produced such difficulties.

For some of the children, too, it was not easy to adapt. In other classes, there were 'right' and 'wrong' answers, and there were good notes to learn at the end of a lesson. If one remembered them and reproduced the appropriate words in a test, good marks were received. Notes with Nuffield were much more dependent on the individual, and the tests were more hypothetical – seeking interpretation of data, ideas for experiments and transfer of knowledge from one piece of practical work to others. Memorising the notes paid few dividends for the children, but understanding the approach and concepts could be very rewarding. That was much harder work!

Many teachers continued with Nuffield successfully, amending and adapting some of the ideas but sustaining the attitude. Some absorbed some of the themes and practical work into their more traditional courses, making them more exciting but losing the attitude that accompanied the activities. Others dropped the system almost entirely, finding the lack of control and authority difficult to accept. However, Nuffield approaches were a considerable stimulant to curriculum thinking. The Nuffield Science scheme was a very large undertaking: three subjects plus integrated science, five-year courses for O level and then two years of A level for Chemistry, Physics and Biology. In 1969, Don Reid and Phil Booth added to the scheme publications to encourage 'individual learning' for O level, which today would be lumped under the heading of 'open learning'. In my school, the conditions were not suitable for a successful introduction of such an approach. At the heart of Nuffield was an attitude to children, to teaching and to the essence of the subjects. When the Schools Council was flourishing in the 1970s it was to similar large schemes that it turned most of its attention, and again it was the attitude, more than the content, that was significant. The trend that ran through them all was the same – the increasing emphasis on the child exploring and discovering his or her own insights and understanding. For them all, there arose similar problems, mainly associated with the role of the teacher within an existing educational environment.

Calculating

One of my other responsibilities at the school was to improve supporting resources for the teachers, which included audio-visual equipment and reprographics. Paper generation has always been an essential aid to teaching, and we were living in the worksheet age.

To keep myself up to date with the latest developments, I visited the Business Efficiency Exhibition at Earls Court in 1968. On one of the stands was a four-function electronic calculator, about twice the size of my hand. There had been a mass of relatively small adding machines, but this one astonished me by its simplicity and ease of use. I felt that major changes in mathematical education would result, until I found out the price – it was £75.

The first programme of computer policy

After two years' work, John Duke, an assistant director of the National Council for Educational Technology, was finally able in June 1969 to complete the feasibility study on the 'Potential applications and development of computer-based learning systems'. The working party that had undertaken the study had met many times, and now a £2m project over five years was being recommended to the Department of Education and Science. The (then) Secretary of State, Margaret Thatcher, agreed to the proposal in the Spring of 1972, and the National Development Programme in Computer Assisted Learning (NDPCAL) was born.

> The aim of the Programme was to develop and secure the assimilation of computer-assisted learning on a regular institutional basis at reasonable cost. Thus, the emphasis of the National Programme would be on development activities leading to continuity of use beyond the period when central funding is involved.
>
> Computer technology can be used in four main ways in educational systems:
>
> 1. as an instrument of research;
> 2. in courses concerned with computer education and computer science;
> 3. in the management of education and its institutions;
> 4. as a medium of teaching and learning in a range of subject areas.
>
> The National Development Programme will concern itself exclusively with the third and fourth categories of use. (NCET, 1973)

This was the brief which faced the Director, Richard Hooper, when he started in January 1973. During its five years, the Programme supported some 35 projects including seven in schools, twelve in tertiary education and eight in armed services training. Projects ranged from development work to feasibility studies and also included examination of the various issues surrounding transferability. Several related to the potential of computer-managed learning, ways in which the student could be guided to various stages of working activity depending on his or her success at various modules of study. These included work on maths and biology in schools, and the possibility of using the system in teacher training. Over the last ten years, interest in this use of the computer has waned, as everybody has been concentrating on its use in learning, but this organisational use is likely to recur as courses become more modular in their approach.

During this period of activity the age of microcomputers had not yet begun, and most of the work was conducted on mainframes, usually with teletype terminals. Most of the study material was therefore text-based, and appeared in context very like programmed learning. Apart from the excitement of working with a computer as a delivery system, the materials lacked many of the motivating characteristics that teachers expected. However, there was an underlying feeling within those involved in the Programme that computers had a great deal to offer in the support of education and training in the future. Costs of hardware were falling, but those for software would continue to rise and Hooper's final report laid stress on this.

The report (Hooper, 1977) identified four characteristics of the computer that would ensure it an important role in the future: its versatility, the academic respectability accorded to computing, its power as a simulator, and the fact that it was part of the industrial and commercial world.

While little was discovered about the potential of computer-assisted learning during the project (largely because the technical conditions were unhelpful), the work laid the foundations for the acceptance of the importance of the technology in the future of education. Several universities and some of the school projects continued, and were important bases from which the next government-sponsored programme could develop. In particular, several significant people had been identified and held office.

Investigating

In 1981, the Cockcroft Report was published, and had a major effect on the planning of the maths curriculum for the GCSE and beyond. Its timing was such that the potential of computers in assisting the learning of maths was hardly addressed, although the importance and value of calculators was strongly noted.

In paragraph 243, Cockcroft states:

Mathematics teaching at all levels should include opportunities for:

- exposition by the teacher;
- discussion between teacher and pupils and between pupils themselves;
- appropriate practical work;
- consolidation and practice of fundamental skills and routines;
- investigational work.

The emphasis on practical and investigational work, long recognised as important but little undertaken in practice, proved to be the basis of much of the new thinking about the approach to the maths curriculum. Children should be exploring number, function and application to develop their understanding, rather than merely acquiring a set of routines to apply. Such routines should emerge as part of the developed wisdom where possible, and their selection should relate to practice in problem solving. Exploring in this way broadened understanding, and the errors that would emerge were as important in furthering knowledge as achieving correct answers.

Difficulties in providing lessons that fostered that approach were considerable. Suitable materials were not familiar to teachers, and their background and tradition did not lead to this form of practice. Writing in the *Times Educational Supplement*, Hugh Burkhardt identified three ways in which this more 'open' teaching style was more demanding on teachers:

1. Mathematically by asking him to discern a pupil's line of argument, diagnose its possibilities and errors, and direct the next stage in a way that builds on the pupil's achievements so far.
2. Pedagogically by asking her to accept and handle a much wider range of problems, and to progress by making use of the different approaches and abilities of individual pupils.
3. Personally by requiring the teacher to have the confidence to follow pupils into areas that he has not himself explored and to admit that there are many things that he doesn't know. (Burkhardt, 1982)

The movement towards overcoming such difficulties is slow and depends on much retraining and the development of new attitudes, but the impetus given by the Cockcroft report to move in this direction has been considerable. As it begins to succeed, so the infection of the attitude will start to spread to other subjects.

Text by television

When Sam Fedida conceived the idea of text being broadcast at the same time as television pictures – the teletext system – he was thinking of the problems of the deaf. Optional subtitles available through special television sets would be a considerable asset for them. So from 1973 on, the BBC started transmitting a text magazine (now called Ceefax) using two of the 'blank' lines between pictures. By 1976 quite a sophisticated service was in operation, and two years later ITV started the similar Oracle pages. When Channel 4 started, the Oracle service was immediately available with its transmissions.

Subtitles were broadcast from the beginning, and gradually the number of programmes for which they were available increased. The preparation of these titles was expensive in terms of labour, but gradually the technology made this a faster process. Simultaneous titling, however, remains difficult.

While the technique and information was exciting for those able to afford the more expensive sets, initial public response was not very enthusiastic. However, part of the IT82 (Information Technology Year, as promoted by the Department of Trade and Industry) publicity was support for these teletext systems, and the growth of sales began to rise.

This support was also directed towards the British Telecom Prestel system, although the service began when the company was part of the Post Office in 1979. Often linked with teletext because both provide an information service, Prestel is very different technically, being a viewdata system requiring cable connection to the television set through telephone circuits.

The broadcast teletext service is essentially free to the user, offering access to selected pages that are broadcast repeatedly alongside the transmissions. There is no feedback to the broadcasters, except through other methods of communication. In contrast, the viewdata service provides pages of information at the customer's request, each of which can carry a charge. While pages can be, and usually are, just viewed or downloaded into the user's computer, direct interaction with the Prestel mainframe can take place as the two are interlinked through the system.

Marketing the Prestel service proved a difficult task and for several years the number of subscribers was low. Education took an early interest, and the Council for Educational Technology (became National Council for Educational Technology (NCET) on 1 April, 1988) supported investigations into various ways of selecting and collating references to a range of pages of information that could support curriculum activity. The Council was also much involved in determining the protocols that should be used in storing computer programs on the Prestel system so that they could be downloaded into school equipment and used by the teachers and children. These protocols proved to be the standard for both this work and programs which the service began to offer later for the home user.

Downloading computer programs through a direct link such as Prestel was more obvious than receiving them from broadcasts. However, when Acorn announced the first BBC computer in 1981, such a teletext service was envisaged. The initial equipment that was provided to receive the pages was awkward to use and somewhat unreliable, but later improvements have since made the reception of broadcast teletext an increasingly simple activity. Through funding made available by the Microelectronics Education Programme, the BBC was able to employ a member of staff to develop a computer program distribution service, and this has proved technically effective.

Both teletext and viewdata services have expanded since, and now offer the foundation of considerable information sources. Prestel was once described as the 'people's database' - presumably because its target was to carry general information - but it now has specialised areas for particular audiences. The education area is growing in depth and value, and its operators are continually striving to find material of curricular relevance. In theory the database is infinitely extensive, yet one of its major roles is seen to be that of acting as a gateway to other systems that extend and specialise the information available on the main system.

Access to Prestel is dependent on wired connections, and in the UK the telephone system is sufficiently extensive to ensure that this is possible everywhere. To recable to carry all the video and data channels that futurologists foresee is an expensive investment. In rural areas it is unlikely to be cost-effective, and in many parts of the world it appears that such a system may take many years to be installed. For social and democratic reasons such a venture may be considered important, but it is likely to be delayed by economic reality.

Some of the needs may be met by expansion of the present broadcast systems. The current limitations on the area covered by present television transmissions are overcome by the use of satellites, so larger audiences could use such a data distribution system. Devoting more transmission lines or even whole frames to this service, particularly during the night, could enlarge the capacity of the system enormously. Coupled with automatic reception and capturing of the data, such a system could prove to be a very efficient updating and world news service, as well as distributing software originals and revisions. Early moves towards this are the Datacast service of the BBC and a similar option from Independent television.

Teletext is now widely used by the general public, and although at present the viewdata service is not taken by such a large audience its technology is well-proven. Between them, the two systems offer people access to a range of programs and updated supporting data, as well as providing the opportunity to explore and question an increasingly extensive range of information.

Debating

In 1976 at Ruskin College, Oxford the (then) Prime Minister, James Callaghan, gave a speech on education on 18 October which was to initiate the Great Debate. Meetings and seminars were held around the country in the next two years to explore the purpose and organisation of education, but the Debate itself never really started. Many people aired their prejudices but little was actually debated. Attending one such meeting was a disillusioning experience, with poorly-briefed civil servants giving inadequate statements that missed most of the salient issues that confronted the curriculum.

One theme of disquiet that emerged there and elsewhere was a failure to prepare children for the world of industry and commerce. For many years industry has complained about education, but frequently with contradictory voices. Too often education was expected to be the panacea for industrial failure, and schools were encouraged to provide an education mainly geared to commercial needs.

During the Great Debate these themes were reiterated, and it became clear that in many people's eyes the purpose of education was to prepare young people for work. Commenting later on this, two Labour MPs, Ivor Clemitson and George Rodgers, wrote:

Of course it is true that industry needs skill. Indeed as technology advances it will be skilled rather than unskilled labour that will be required, and the kind of skills demanded will change rapidly. There is, therefore, a great need for an expansion of training and retraining facilities, and for there to be ample scientists and technologists of high standard. But to thrust this into the central place in the educational debate is to misread the changing role of employment in society, and to miss the great opportunities which that change makes possible for human welfare and development. If education for children and young people is about preparing them for life, then it must be preparation for full life, and not merely for employment. What has always been desirable is now not only becoming possible but, more than that, essential if young people are to be prepared to take up the possibilities of the new age. In the fruitful transition to that new age education has an obviously vital role to play. (Clemitson and Rodgers, 1981)

The Great Debate raised the position of education in the political arena but failed to explore the issues that would be at the heart of the problems in the decades leading to the next century. Involving parents in such discussions is very important; however, they must be properly briefed on the subject for debate and not left to rely on their memories of their own education, which naturally took place in an entirely different kind of society. The relationship of education to industry is one that continues to perplex and cause much unease.

The micros are coming

In 1977 I was offered, in a postal competition, the chance to win a new PET computer as a prize. This was the first time I had seen a fully constructed microcomputer so advertised. For the enthusiastic hobbyist who was also a dab hand with a soldering machine, kits had been available since 1975, but it was the arrival of the PET machine that launched the deluge. Memory and processing power in those early days were small, and for storage there was the cassette recorder. But even with these limitations, the dream for education in the future was beginning to form.

That early PET and the more versatile Apple that followed shortly afterwards provided many ideas for the teachers who first played with them. Programming was tedious and restricted; colour was missing and graphics were chunky and unreal; putting cards into the Apple introduced some simple sounds; imaginative links to electronic apparatus introduced some primitive control work. Already available in a few local education authorities was the early version of the Research Machines 380Z, built to withstand the worst school treatment that could be imagined.

Educational use at this time was still linked mainly to the programmed learning approach. Text was churned out on the screen, but was very hard to read as it was often in capital letters and with little space between lines. Responses by the pupil were usually limited to numbers, grid references and 'yes/no' answers. A few programs offered pupils the opportunity to try out a change of parameter, for example the position of windmills on an island or the size of a box representing an animal, but these were very much the exception. In Hatfield, Bill Tagg had recognised the importance of databases for any educational work and had begun developing one for the Research Machines computer.

Even if the machines lacked sophistication and power, they allowed interested teachers to explore and test their imagination. Soon, more memory and processing power would arrive (and it did much more quickly than most people expected) – then the ideas which were currently frustrated would be capable of realisation. Simply achievable at the time were programs that practised memorisation or fundamental skills such as multiplication tables, and these were written by many different people. For those who were apprehensive about the arrival of these machines, such applications confirmed their worst fears; later developments were constantly criticised from the memory of these early trials.

Technically, there has been considerable growth in the ten years since the arrival of these early machines and the cost to education has fallen, taking the changing value of money into account. Yet the speed of the present school microcomputer, its internal and external memory capacity, and the facilities that it offers have all expanded enormously. Colour, graphics, a range of languages, easier programming, and a substantial array of tools, utilities and subject-based software are now part of the package which is expected with this technology. Apple, the company that introduced one of the first machines, has proved particularly innovative in its developments, devising the 'mouse' and the concept of windows and pull-down menus that have now become standard requirements on most computers. The hypercard software that they introduced in 1987 is the beginning of the next round of integrated software environments that will dominate future developments. Innovations like these change considerably the facilities that can be used by those who develop educational programs, and thus expand the opportunities available to learners in addressing information and exploring its meaning. Without these new technical developments, the environment that the computer offers would be more limited and would restrict the learning styles that can be used. Liaison and co-operation between educators and those responsible for technical progress is invaluable if learners are going to be able to make the best use of the opportunities that the technology can provide. Research Machines in particular, but Acorn also, have been keen to foster such a dialogue in this country, and have reaped a high proportion of the educational market as a result.

The future is beckoning

'Horizon' has always been a noteworthy BBC television programme, dealing in depth and at a serious level with one scientific or technical topic per transmission. In March 1978, one of the programmes was called 'Now the Chips are Down'. It has long been rumoured that the (then) Prime Minister, James Callaghan, watched this description of silicon chips, their potential and some of the possible social consequences that would follow from their use, and ordered a general enquiry throughout government departments on what was being prepared to exploit them and prepare for their impact. Whether or not the story is true, the broadcast was followed by a great wave of interest. Articles, books, speeches and various media activities took place in large numbers during the next two years. Magazines on the subject were launched, and, while many have foundered since, some (such as *Personal Computer World*) have continued to prosper.

In France, the President had been anxious about the issue some 15 months earlier. In December 1976 Giscard D'Estaing had appointed a Commission under Simon Nora to prepare a report on 'L'Informatisation de la société'; written with Alain Minc, it was published in France in January 1978. This report was extremely popular as it addressed the issues that would confront a society enjoying the widespread use of computers. Interestingly, the report dealt mainly with the impact on political structures, the difficulties that would face government when the public had much greater access to information. The potential for decentralisation was considerable, and Nora argued for a government policy directed towards achieving a balance between sovereign (that is, central) prerogatives and those undertaken at the periphery.

On the matter of unemployment, the report suggested that 'the service industries will release personnel while large industrial enterprises will expand with a constant level of employment'. Not appreciated in the report was the growth of the new service activities which more than mopped up the labour that was released in this area. Nora launched a substantial attack on the domination of American companies, and urged major government investment in schemes to promote computerisation – in particular in communications. Education received only a small mention, but the report stated:

> Specialisation will fade away and levels of teaching will become diversified, modifying the rigid statutory requirements on which diplomas and grades are based. Education will see its function distilled to one of coordination, while more routine tasks will be carried out by assistants. (Nora and Minc, 1980)

The Nora report was the most authoritative government publication on the impact of these technologies produced at the time. However, there were many other documents – the theme of unemployment and job reorganisation being the dominant issue. This featured largely in Barron and Curnow's (1979) book *The Future with Microelectronics*, the nearest to the Nora report that was produced in the United Kingdom. Surveying the changes in technology as well as those in society, the authors' conclusions included urging the government to create an Institute of Information Technology.

Like all the writing at this time, there was much informed guessing as to the expected effects of the technology on society in general and on industry in particular. Jenkins and Sherman (1979) received considerable publicity for their book *The Collapse of Work* as they forecast considerable increases in unemployment to over three million during the next decade. Running through their chapters was the suggestion for more government intervention to ensure that our industries would be prepared to develop and exploit the new technologies; otherwise we would become a substantial net importer with consequent effects on jobs. Unfortunately this is now the position of our economy.

At a more popular level, and backed by a television series, the late Dr Chris Evans (1979) published *The Mighty Micro*. This also concentrated on industrial change, unemployment and access to information, but included sections on gimmicks and gadgets. My favourite remains the 'portable book', a rechargeable liquid crystal screen into which one inserts a ROM chip on which is stored the text. Thus bookshops and libraries do not deal in paper books but in ROM chips for the ubiquitous 'portable reader'.

Another text that had a considerable effect on educators was *The Micro Revolution* (Peter Large, 1980). The author was a journalist on *The Guardian* and extracts in the paper had attracted attention. Of particular interest was the first chapter, written in the form of science fiction, describing a journalist preparing her story on the beach. Seemingly far-fetched and extraordinary, Peter Large revealed that all the technology the journalist used was currently available.

Even more influential was a paper given by Professor William Gosling in May 1978 to a small conference of organisations interested in educational technology. Organised by the Council for Educational Technology, the paper was called 'The kingdom of sand'. Professor Gosling's 'sand' encompassed the silicon in microelectronic chips and in the glass of optical fibres, and the talk highlighted briefly the salient changes that would affect society, including the reorganisation of employment. Educationists, he claimed, must be concerned with this technology for

... all education, by its nature [is] preoccupied with that very business of storing, retrieving and disseminating information upon which the microelectronics age will have its most immediate and rapid impact ... Jobs will disappear and others gain new importance, and the outcome will bear little relationship to the status and esteem in which the same jobs are held at the present time. Only a seer could predict the whole pattern, yet paradoxically in education we must prepare for it. All we can do is cling to the belief that now, more than ever in history, we must be flexible not only in our educational methods but even in goals. We must ever be prepared to devise new kinds of educational experiences and abandon old ones. Above all we must avoid the adoption of oganisational structures or, and this is particularly important, educational technologies which tend to congeal patterns of teaching and learning into forms not easily changed.

The paper ends with the memorable statement:

'In the kingdom of sand all things become possible, and only imagination rules.' (Gosling, 1978)

Following this paper, the Council prepared several persuasive documents that urged the Department of Education and Science to launch further projects to ensure that microelectronics was exploited at all levels of education. Combined with the Whitehall review stimulated by the Prime Minister, this pressure led to the funding of the Microelectronics Education Programme and an atmosphere in government that considered support for information technology to be a 'good thing'.

No selective review of the influential activity in these years would be complete without mention of Professor Tom Stonier. During this time and through the years that followed he was the guru of the media, writing and speaking widely in an attempt to attract attention to the importance of seizing the initiative and exploiting opportunities before others took them from us. Some of his addresses, compellingly presented, appeared to overstate a case that the public in general found difficult to accept as real anyway. Education was being faced with contraction and smaller funds, and his plea that the future was dependent on greater investment fell on already deaf ears. Nevertheless the argument was cogently given. Employment in manufacturing industries would fall, and needed to be taken up in the knowledge industries where the future of society's wealth lay.

The most sensible and logical way to do this is through a massive expansion of the education system, because the education system is, first of all, labour-intensive in its own right, and could produce hundreds of thousands of jobs; secondly it would help keep many of the young people who comprise the bulk of the unemployed off the labour market, or draw them back into the education system; and thirdly the upgrading of the UK's knowledge base would allow it to devise new industries which would produce the wealth from which the government could draw its revenues to pay for the whole thing (Stonier, 1979).

These themes were developed extensively later in his book *The Wealth of Information*. (Stonier, 1983)

Imports are not the answer

In 1980 an experiement was taking place in the West Midlands, sponsored by Control Data Corporation and using a network of terminals linked to a mainframe. The software was American, the purpose basic education. The user operated the program through a touch screen, and was able to move items around from one part to another.

For British children it proved a failure, as the programs were all 'drill and practice' in design and (in spite of some interesting graphics) failed to motivate them for very long. While the programs proved interesting for slow learners, those with more ability soon tired of them. At one time, a project was suggested that would use an authoring system for software that would be more appropriate for British education, but the costs were far too large to be acceptable to local education authorities. Later, the programming system 'Tutor' became available on stand-alone microcomputers, but even then the costs were too high for British education and they were not taken up.

Other efforts have been made to adapt some of the large number of programs made for American education. Even though most were written for the Apple, conversion was not seen to be a major problem if the quality and approach proved appropriate. Those that were seen up to 1984 failed to prove acceptable, as they were predominantly 'drill and practice' in design and did not match the more open and exploratory approach that dominated British schools. However exciting or interesting the graphics, the target of the programs was to teach memorisation rather than understanding, and this in the end proved boring to children. Directed towards a system that placed high regard on passing tests at each grade – tests that were dependent predominantly on good recall – these programs had proved in practice to be well researched and successfully applied. However, under the very different circumstances of British education, they did not fit.

In 1985, I received a number of reports that American teachers were putting their microcomputers away as they were bored with them. Was this a movement against technology as an aid for learning, or was it the software they were using?

Why have micros in school?

What was the purpose of the computer in education, particularly in schools? In tertiary education, it was clearly valuable administratively and as an information storage system, as well as a mechanism that students studied for degrees in computer science and electronics. Did the same apply to schools?

By 1980, the debate was taking place as if these were opposite camps. There were strong advocates for computer studies as a subject for children. Since 1974 computer studies had become more and more popular, and by 1981 over 15,000 children were taking it at O level and many more at CSE, usually using locally devised syllabuses. Hampered initially by lack of equipment, many children had made use of a terminal attached to the local authority, polytechnic or university mainframe computer which arrived at periodic intervals in their schools. Microcomputers raised the possibility of having continuous practical work available, and this was a considerable advantage.

Repeated exposure in the media gave the computer a high profile; at a time when employment problems were beginning to look difficult, parents saw this field as one in which their children should be able to prosper. That school computer studies was not accepted as a valid qualification for entry into this field did not deter their enthusiasm for supporting the subject.

In local education authorities some advisers had been appointed to co-ordinate and maintain standards in the subject, and these people became spokesmen for sustaining support for the subject. The apparent opposite camp consisted of those who advocated the use of the computer across the curriculum, seeing it as a valuable teaching aid for every subject rather than merely located in computer studies. Like so many such debates in education, it was a false conflict from the start. Those supporting computer studies also felt that there was considerable potential in using appropriate software for learning in the rest of the curriculum, while those urging the wider use of the equipment felt there was a place for the special subject.

The origin of the debate rotated around funding and the availability of equipment. Spurred on by civil servants desperately hunting for priorities, questions were raised to identify whether the small number of machines that a school would have should go to the computer studies area or to the whole school. Important as this appeared for administrators, the practical outcome in the school ignored their views and relied, as they always do, on the personal choices of head teachers, advisers, teachers and children. Thus, in some schools computer studies gained equipment while in others it was dispersed to subject areas. The issue became even more unimportant when in the following few years microcomputers were acquired in considerable numbers and were spread in all directions.

More difficult were the conflicting roles of advisers. Most LEAs had staff appointed as educational technology advisers, who were responsible for audio, film and video and usually for reprographics too, and who also promoted educational technology in teaching and learning in their schools. The arrival of microcomputers raised difficult questions of responsibility. If there was a strong adviser for computer studies, were the microcomputers his responsibility? If the LEA wished to persuade a broader across-the-curriculum approach, should they not be the responsibility of the educational technology adviser? Surely, too, the microcomputer and associated developments were very important elements in the armoury of educational technology in the future. Finally, there was the place of control technology as it developed from the computer. Whose responsibility was this?

Once again, there was great variability among LEAs. In some, all the responsibility was taken by the computer adviser; in some, by the educational technology adviser; in others by the adviser for craft, design and technology. Depending on the person some aspects were promoted at the expense of others, but the pervasive nature of the computer in its applications was clearly reflected in these difficulties. In some places a new name was given to the adviser, for example 'responsible for information technology', to try to define the role more accurately.

For some people, responsibility for media studies was included as part of the activity. This developed from work with film and video as a natural extension of the role, but as a subject it sat uncomfortably, having closer affinity to the approach of English and literature. However, it was felt that the appearance of information technology had begun to alter many of the concepts within media studies, and this has been proved by recent developments such as desk-top publishing.

Thus, by the middle of the 1980s, advisers with responsibility for computers in their LEAs were variously found with different mixtures of the following areas as part of their brief: information technology, educational technology, film, video, resource-based learning, media studies, control technology, craft, design and technology, physics, mathematics, TVEI, and computer studies. Considering that many of these advisers came from personal teaching backgrounds in geography and biology as well as physics and mathematics, the diversity of experience has proved considerable.

Vocational education

One of the difficulties facing the Secretary of State for Education is the independent role of the local education authorities. It is they who have ultimate responsibility for disposing resources and also for the curriculum in their schools, while the Secretary of State can merely urge and advise. Changes in the rules surrounding the dispersal of funds have now given the Secretary of State some authority to hold back part of the funds under the rate support grant and direct its dispersal in a targetted fashion. Money allocated from this source - the ESG (Educational Supplementary Grants) - is directed towards particular needs, for example the purchase of specific equipment and in-service training in particular areas. While these targets are agreed by the local education authorities, and the funding for particular projects are supplemented from their own sources in most cases, they are selected by the Secretary of State.

These rules were not changed in 1982, and the frustration of government was evident. Growing levels of unemployment, a lack of appropriate skilled manpower and the apparent unpreparedness of school-leavers for industry and entrepreneurial activities were all anxieties which were troubling Ministers. However, acting through directly targetted money soon presented difficulties for the Department of Education and Science. Such constraints, though, did not affect organisations like the Manpower Services Commission, and thus it was this body, and the enthusiasm of Lord Young (then David Young), that launched the TVEI (Technical and Vocational Educational Initiative) scheme with an announcement by the Prime Minister in November that year. Every LEA has now joined the scheme, although not every school is yet involved. While initially targetted at 15-year-olds and upwards, many Initiatives now involve younger children. The extension is planned to affect all 14- to 18-year-olds by 1992.

The aim of the scheme was to increase job-related education, and to do this through ideas and initiatives conceived by teachers and LEAs that were then approved by the Commission. It was categorically aimed not at lower ability children (although many thought of it this way) but at the whole range. In practice, the proportion of children with a potential of three A levels involved in the scheme has been small. The guidelines included requirements to concentrate on both sexes; provide a four-year course encouraging initiative, problem-solving ability and personal development; involve work experience; and ensure good counselling, career guidance and a general and technical and vocational education. As far as the schools were concerned, there was added income in a substantial form to support the acquisition of resources for the work, and also funds for staff at both school and LEA level.

At the educational level, in the absence of a defined curriculum there was the opportunity for imaginative teachers and schools to use the Initiative to begin to undertake interesting curriculum development. For example, there was considerable growth in modular learning, and in some schools this has developed into fully supported self-study techniques. Emerging in schools that are strongly committed to the scheme is a breakdown of traditional subject areas and a growth of interdisciplinary work. The subject matter incorporated into TVEI has always been broad, from business studies and modified home economics on one hand to design and technology on the other but, by taking the vocational aspect as a major criterion, elements of a wide range of subject matter including languages and mathematics, English and applied geography, begin to find a place.

The effect of the Initiative has been considerable, principally because it brought substantial extra funds and a freedom of action that stimulated change and innovation. The outcomes have often been exciting for children and have extended their areas of learning in new ways; even more importantly they have opened up new thinking about the content and approaches adopted in the curriculum.

The second programme of computer policy

When James Callaghan pursued his interest in 'Now the Chips are Down' into the Department of Education and Science, Shirley Williams (who was then Secretary of State) was also receiving advice from other quarters, not the least from Geoffrey Hubbard at the Council for Educational Technology. The response of the Department was to announce a five-year programme on 6 March 1979 funded at £12m over five years. A similar programme was announced in Scotland, and started quickly, but that of the Department of Education and Science was still undergoing the consultancy period when the election of June 1979 was announced. The external consultations ended in April, but the officials were still considering how to go forward. Enterprising colleges and individuals had sent in proposals based on the initial announcement, but nothing happened as the country voted and changed the government.

The new incumbents considered at length the ideas of their predecessors and it was not until 4 March 1980 that the (then) Minister of State, Neil Macfarlane, announced a new programme – now only £9m spread over four years. The remit was roughly the same, new materials to include software, teacher training and broad initiatives being the main themes. I was appointed as Director in July, commenced work in November and published my strategy for the programme in March 1981. This was one year after the announcement, and left only three years in which to complete the programme. Called the Microelectronics Education Programme (MEP), it was extended for a further two years until March 1986, following a decision announced in March 1983, and involved some £23m in total by the time it was closed. To complete the story, its closure was announced (June 1985) at the same time as the formation of a replacement organisation – the Microelectronics Education Support Unit. However, it took the Department until May 1986 to appoint a Director; it was September when he officially started and January 1987 when the staff to do the work finally took up their posts. Then, a year later in January 1988, the Department decided to amalgamate this Unit with the Council for Educational Technology and once again flooded the organisation with indecision and uncertainty.

At the end of the 1970s the field of microelectronics was not widely taught at school, and thus the development of the Strategy took place against a background where advice and experience were in short supply. On the one hand were those with a computer science background promoting in particular the further development of computer studies, while in the other camp were those who foresaw a broad curricular impact and wished to see that advanced. Again, this was more an academic than a real conflict, although it reared its head on occasions when there was a debate over particular resources. What was significant about the Programme was the breadth of its interest, craft, design and technology and computer science for those with technical interests, business studies for those with the modern office in view and computer-based learning materials for all subjects. There was also a strand of development work examining the changing perspective on information and a range of activity in the field of special education.

Organisationally, the Programme was permeated through regional activities based around 14 centres that required liaison between the local LEAs. It was heavily dependent on joint activities: with LEAs on training and development; with industry and publishers on the preparation, publication and distribution of materials; with tertiary education on the support of innovative developments. Through such collaborations, MEP trebled the money that was spent on the work, introduced the ideas to a wide range of participants and ensured the continuation of some of its initiatives after it finished.

Its remit made clear that there would be no support for hardware purchases – all the budget would be spent on training and development. While accepting that this was a viable approach which was understandable at a time when funds were short, it did mean that teachers who had received some training and even software might return to their schools and find no equipment on which to exploit their new expertise.

Writing as an ordinary backbench MP in *The Guardian* on the last day of 1980, Kenneth Baker stated that there was a mass of advertisements in the local press for wordprocessor operators, programmers and system analysts. Not enough was being done at school to train the next generation, he claimed, particularly as children were fascinated by the new technology. Having criticised his Government's programme of £9m as woefully inadequate, he made four recommendations:

Within a year or 18 months every secondary school should have a microcomputer … Several teachers from each school should undergo a Computer-Assisted Learning course in the techniques and usage of computers … The aim should be that within three years every boy and girl who leaves school should be familiar with computers and associated technology, and have acquired a simple digital facility and some experience in using and understanding them … The attitude of careers advisers should be transformed so that they don't always recommend their brightest pupils to study pure science for there are more than enough unemployed physicists and chemists. These children should be encouraged to study computer sciences. (Baker, 1980)

Within a few weeks of writing this, the Prime Minister promoted Kenneth Baker to a Ministerial post in the Department of Trade and Industry, and the civil servants began to prepare a 'Micros in Schools' scheme. This was geared to giving the value of half the price of a microcomputer to every secondary school, and after some persuasion financial support through MEP to assist in training two teachers per school in basic familiarisation. By the end of 1982, 15 months after the scheme started, almost every secondary school had one microcomputer. This was followed by a similar scheme for primary schools which ended in 1984 with nearly all having a machine, the training this time being through a pack and limited tutorial sessions as the numbers were so large. In August 1983 the DTI were giving away more equipment to secondary schools, helping them with devices and upgrading. Teacher training establishments also received a donation of equipment, and in 1985 the DTI announced a scheme that would help schools to purchase software. Further activity followed: a modem scheme, desk-top publishing and computer-assisted design equipment, as well as considerable support for a development project on 'Interactive Video in Schools' which produced eight discs for trialling and evaluation.

Given the substantial funds of the TVEI scheme that were being provided by the Manpower Services Commission and the additional considerable activity from the DTI, the resources that the Department of Education and Science were providing through MEP seemed very small. The initiative in education seemed to be almost anywhere but in its own department.

However, the DTI schemes solved the MEP problem of equipment in schools, and gave the Programme a chance to provide teachers with materials for which there were some machines (however few) available. MEP worked at both primary and secondary levels, introducing teachers of all subjects to the potential of software. Other important aspects of its activities included the promotion and support of control technology and materials for courses in microelectronics, the use of the technology in special education, and the establishment of information studies as a major area of concern in any curriculum in the future. There were also projects in computer studies, helping to update the approach and content of the subject and provide a selection of learning materials.

Just as users expected computers to produce instant answers to all questions, so hopes were high that the technology would prove itself to be the quick answer to educational problems. Yet, during the life of the Programme, the equipment remained relatively primitive and available in schools only in very small quantities. What was undertaken was an examination through experiment and observation of the potential educational benefits that the computer could provide, most of them unachievable until the processing power, memory, design and peripherals were developed much further.

Early use had shown that drill and practice software was of limited application but that, especially in special education, it had a place in the repertoire of resources that a teacher could use. Much more searching and valuable were the more exploratory programs, which set learners along avenues of discovery and experiment that inspired and cultivated curiosity. Together with tools such as wordprocessors and databases, these programs provided the basis for a range of activities that could change approaches and attitudes to learning and indeed the position and role of teachers. At no time was there any thought that the computer would become the only source through which learning would take place - merely that here was an instrument that would be an additional resource through which children could be helped to learn.

Compared with the rest of the world, Britain started early and developed acceptance and integration into its schools further than any other country in 1986. While there were many more computers in American schools by that date their use was relatively limited, and the programs that American teachers were using were very largely confined to the drill and practice area. Since MEP closed, in other countries – particularly Canada, Australia and within Europe – considerable strides have been taken in incorporating the computer into the school environment and using a wide variety of programs. Regrettably, investment in new developments in software has virtually ceased in Britain, the emphasis being on consolidation of the present position in order to ensure that a wider range of teachers in more schools make use of the resources already available.

The curriculum debate continues

The 1980s have seen a surge of interest in the school curriculum, accompanied by numerous publications from the Department of Education and Science. Many of these have come from the hands of Her Majesty's Inspectorate (HMI), some as government guidelines. Since the oil crisis, and the Prime Minister's speech at Ruskin College, debate about the content of the school curriculum has gathered apace. In part, this results from a feeling that children leaving school are not able to support the industrial and commercial world that they are to enter. While it is true that many do not have the detailed skills that this world requires, most are not the skills that a school would be expected to teach anyway. Some schools have responded to the demand for office skills by purchasing IBM computers and office software so that the children will have learned their typing with the same wordprocessors that they will find in the businesses they may eventually join. That offices will have replaced these machines by others within a few years makes a nonsense of such a policy, but it reflects the desire to supply commerce with children who have exactly the right background.

Much of the industrial issue is not related to the capabilities or lack of skills of the school-leaver but rather to the education of those who are ten or more years older than they, those responsible for managerial decisions rather than the new entrants. There has been a well-documented absence of training and support for upgrading the skills and knowledge of employees in British industry, and significant difficulties in matching company direction to economic and commercial realities. These are not issues that are the responsibility of the school-leaver.

Nevertheless, a ferment of publications has occurred because the nature of the school curriculum is now a major political and social issue. From *A Framework for the School Curriculum* (DES, 1980), the HMI red books *A View of the Curriculum* (HMI, 1980), *The School Curriculum* (DES, 1981), the White Paper *Better Schools* (DES, 1985) and the series of documents under the general title *Curriculum Matters* (HMI, 1984 onwards), together with others, the DES has gradually moved towards the promotion and acceptance of a formalised core curriculum that has reached the designation of about 70 per cent of available school time through the Education Bill of 1988. The central dictation of the curriculum by government is contrary to the tradition of local responsibility that has pervaded education for the last 100 years. There is also a political argument that postulates that schools are almost irresponsibly devious in the planning of the work that children learn, but this ignores the obsequious way in which they have devised their approach to meet the needs of children wishing to succeed in examinations. The Boards that run exams have protested variety and competition, and indeed allowed locally prepared Mode 3 syllabuses, but in practice through their activity there has been a centrally approved curriculum ever since the Butler Act.

In their *Curriculum Matters* series, HMI for the most part examined the trends of content and approach that they felt were most appropriate for the future. While that for English fell into some difficulties and was substantially rewritten, the rest have matched the feelings of most teachers committed to their particular subject. One booklet, however – *Curriculum Matters 2* – stood out as markedly different, for it referred to no specific subject but rather to those issues that pervade learning in all areas. Apparently published against some opposition, the booklet follows lines that are much closer to those academics advocating a curriculum based around skills and attitudes than the government enthusiasm for subjects. Nevertheless, the booklet accepts the existence of this direction.

> The overall curricular framework is viewed from two essential and complementary perspectives; first, areas of learning and experience and second, elements of learning, that is, the knowledge, concepts, skill and attitudes to be developed. These perspectives are not in conflict with the ways in which

schools commonly organise teaching and learning; topics, themes or subjects need to support some or all of the facets of the 'whole education' which the two perspectives describe in helping to achieve the school's aims and objectives. (HMI, 1985)

... And a new learning system

The other significant trend in the curriculum debate has been the pressure towards increasing the autonomy of the learner. There is growing interest in the use of open learning as a system for increasing access to educational opportunity for adults, the most recent realisation of this being the Open College. Less publicised but with many more students are the wide range of correspondence courses and use of open learning in training. All rely on the students taking significant responsibility for their own learning - one element of the concept of autonomy. Much progress has been made in using similar systems in schools through a project known as supported self-study.

In 1981, Philip Waterhouse, a former secondary school headteacher, began a project for the Council for Educational Technology to try to resolve the problems arising from falling rolls and the shortage of subject specialists which threatened the breadth of A-level teaching. Supported-self study was the solution proposed, emphasising the individual nature of learning. As Philip Waterhouse (1983) pointed out frequently, supported self-study is not a delivery system for packages of learning materials. Of course, they are a necessary adjunct, but even more important are the tutors and peers that guide and encourage learning. Waterhouse claims four concepts are developed through the system: autonomy, individualisation, personal relationships, and learning to learn - all of considerable importance for children in the future.

The system was devised for A level, but experience in many schools across the country has shown its value with children of much younger ages. Teachers need to be trained to adapt to the new roles that are necessary if the system is to be successful, and there is a strong challenge to the shape of the school organisation as well.

Although this is essentially a system, an approach to organising learning, it raises the possibility of treating the curriculum differently and exploring different topics. Separating system and technique totally from content prevents one from appreciating that new ways of examining subject matter create a new shape to that which can be learned and introduce the possibility of new topics. This means that the curriculum can be different because new opportunities for learning are on offer. While rightly the new technologies are considered in the first place as tools for the teacher and child to use, their existence introduces new possibilities which were not available before and which therefore open up the potential within the curriculum.

This is the theme of this book: looking at the potential within the curriculum against the background of technical progress and development in educational thinking that has been illustrated, very selectively, in this first part.

References

Baker, K (1980) Now is the time for the microchip kid *Guardian* (31.12.80) London

Barron, I (1979) and Curnow, R *The Future with Microelectronics* Frances Pinter Ltd, London

Broderick, W R (1968) *The Computer in School* Bodley Head, London

Burkhardt, H (1982) Missing classroom activities *Times Education Supplement* (22.10.82, p29) London

Clemitson, I (1981) and Rodgers, G *A Life to Live* Junction Books, London

Cockcroft, W (1981) *Mathematics Counts: The Cockcroft Report* HMSO, London

Department of Education and Science (1980) *A Framework for the School Curriculum* HMSO, London

Department of Education and Science (1981) *The School Curriculum* HMSO, London

Department of Education and Science (1985) *Better Schools* HMSO, London

Evans, C (1979) *The Mighty Micro* Victor Gollancz, London

Gosling, W (1978) 'The kingdom of sand'. In *Microcircuits, Society and Education* CET, London

HMI (1980) *A View of the Curriculum* HMSO, London

HMI (1985) *The Curriculum from 5 to 16. Curriculum Matters 2.* HMSO, London

Hooper, R (1977) *The Final Report of the Director* CET, London

Jenkins, C (1979) and Sherman, B *The Collapse of Work* Eyre Methuen Ltd, London

Large, P (1980) *The Micro Revolution* Fontana paperback, London

Nora, S (1980) and Minc, A *The Computerisation of Society* MIT Press, Cambridge, Massachusetts (English translation)

NCET (1973) *Educational Technology: Progress and Promise* NCET, London

Nuffield (1966) *Biology: Teachers Guide III* Longman/Penguin, London

Stonier, T (1979) paper given at Middlesex Polytechnic January 1979, reprinted in Forester, T (ed) (1980) *The Microelectronics Revolution* Basil Blackwell, Oxford

Stonier, T (1983) *The Wealth of Information* Thames Methuen, London

Waterhouse, P (1983) *Supported Self Study in Secondary Education* CET, London

Part 2

Implications for Today's Curriculum

Chapter 1

Vocational Implications

Introduction

During the last ten years there has been an increasing criticism of schools, focused on the assumed failure of leavers to meet the requirements of industry, business and commerce. Those requirements have rarely been clearly specified, although a great deal of comment has been directed towards illiteracy and innumeracy, the level of which has probably not varied very much since the war. As the country, and most of the Western world, has passed through severe economic tensions and difficulties, much of the implied responsibility has been passed to the education system.

The response has been a growing concern with vocational education. While there has been disagreement about what this phrase actually means, schools have taken more notice of such subjects as business studies and technology as these are easily identified as areas which could have a direct relationship to future employment. Pressure from concerned parents has also been influential in encouraging changes of emphasis in schools, as the type and scarcity of jobs has made it more imperative to ensure that the curriculum at school increases the opportunity for employment.

Much that schools can offer in subjects such as those mentioned above goes only a short distance in providing the skills needed by industry and commerce. Certainly a useful background can be provided and the level of interest raised. However, just as in the 1960s welding in technical schools only led to apprenticeship, now the technological knowledge only encourages an enthusiasm which has to be further developed at college or in the working environment or through personal study, for example by means of some form of open learning. Thus the preparation of children to seek and gain from this further study is as essential a part of their work in school as is the subject matter of the course itself.

Using the equipment

When I was visiting the United States in 1985, I was asked frequently by teachers and journalists at what age we in Britain expected children to be able to touch-type. It was a topic of much debate in that country, and they were eager for advice. The answer I gave was that, apart from those who wished to pursue a career as wordprocessor operators, there did not seem much point to the skill. This created some astonishment among people who were seeking an answer of much less than 10 years old.

Such are the changes and developments to the technology and to input systems like keyboards that it still seems to me a considerable waste of time for the majority of children. That they must be comfortable and relaxed with the equipment of information technology is a prerequisite for living in this age and essential for the future, but touch-typing is not a necessary part of this.

Whether or not children have microcomputers at home they are surrounded by the gadgetry of this technology, and for the most part have little natural fear of it. Some have tension induced by parental anxiety, but most children are unconscious of any problems. Games in cafes, pubs and playcentres are increasingly dependent on electronics and induce no technical anxieties; music and video are part of the young person's environment, again dependent on microelectronics; the bank, telephone, supermarket, transport systems, hospital, are all dependent on information technology for their efficiency and elicit no worries. As children progress through primary school, their familiarity with using the computer should carry them onwards into society in the future with confidence in their ability to use these machines as adeptly and as much like second nature as most secondary school children now use calculators. Gathering information from screens is now the accepted method for transport, in shops, at home, at football grounds, and even in school.

For adults who are meeting this technology from a background of valve radios, the process of becoming comfortable is more difficult. In the early 1980s, it was a common part of the speech of a chief education officer to refer to the computer as something which the children understood but he did not. Such should not be the case now, but in the latter part of 1987 I was surprised to hear the personnel director of a major British technological company almost sounding proud of his continued ignorance.

Even if children are comfortable with the equipment, there is value in some general knowledge of how it works, partly to ensure that they have a broad picture of what is happening as they use it, and partly so that they are aware of the principles behind the various operations they meet in the environment. Children who play computer games or undertake competitive simulations in school rapidly appreciate the idea of a password and the concepts of degrees of privacy, and a few words transfers this to PIN numbers, bank accounts, control of manufacturing systems and personnel databases. Thus, there is no need for lessons about these topics when they can be extrapolated through everyday use.

A broad knowledge of the main parts, processor, input and output, types of memory and links to telephone lines, is useful and can be identified in applications that children meet in their environment. Particularly interesting is the wide range of input sources that can be drawn to their attention as this expands their understanding of the value and limitations of microprocessors. While demonstrating the power and versatility of these devices, such an approach should ensure that the children do not envisage them as miracle machines.

Loading and using software is currently more cumbersome than it will be in the future. Cassettes are now almost forgotten except in the home, and floppy discs in the form that we use at present will soon be of interest to museums only. Learning in detail such mechanisms as these is therefore the acquisition of redundant skills. However, there is a need to cope at the present time, and a few demonstrations will lead most children to a familiarity and confidence that will be sufficient for now. With changes to come, though, the fundamental need is to read instructions, whether on the papers that accompany the material or on the screen. Leaping to conclusions, while fun and intellectually 'macho', will not help when systems and approaches are different. As icons become more popular as guides, interpreting them is not as obvious as many of the designers believe and, for a period, it is likely they will cause much confusion. Only by looking at their meaning will it be possible to use the programs fluently. Before the present primary children finish their compulsory education the whole system will be different again, but reading instructions will continue to be of value.

None of the above matters require special lessons, though it is necessary to ensure they are covered. Carefully planned, and with the time for children to practice and experiment, all the necessary facility and understanding can be acquired as part of the use of the equipment, probably at the primary level. Taking account of external applications and reflecting these to school practice will produce the necessary confidence and ability to meet, and cope and be comfortable with, similar equipment. Keyboard skills will develop in a similar way, through practice and the need to use the equipment. The Qwerty layout is only one keyboard system, and others are and will be present by the time today's children leave school. Initial entry of the text of this book is being done on the six-key Microwriter; modifications will be made through mouse control and a Qwerty keyboard, although if I used a friend's equipment the touch screen would play a significant role. Speech input will probably be the major entry system before the turn of the century, and touch-typing will really be irrelevant. Three years after they asked me the question, I would still give the same answer to those American teachers and journalists.

Technology and computer studies

Because vocational pressure was often related to the need for more engineers and 'computer people', the topics of technology and computer studies were high on the list of subjects to which schools turned. Apart from MEP and the TVEI schemes, the Department of Trade and Industry supported the establishment of British Schools Technology (BST) in 1984, complete with travelling buses, to try to encourage appropriate in-service training and the development of relevant courses. Together the three activities raised the status and recognised importance of technology such that, in the current descriptions of the national curriculum, technology is identified as a part of the core. Unfortunately, many still see it as the core for the less able, pure science being the more academically 'respectable'. Unlike the case in many European countries, the engineer has a comparatively low status – perhaps because the word is so misused – but in our society now and in the future, the importance of good engineers and general engineering skills is considerable if we are to make safe and good use of the technology that is available and create new lines. The products of engineering are important factors in our economic survival.

Computer studies was the subject that raised most attention in the surge of vocationalism, but its continuation is a matter of contentious debate. At the time when there was much publicity about the need for 'computer people', there was a great deal of interest in the subject from children and parents as it appeared to be an entrée into almost guaranteed work. In practice the courses were not designed for this, and while they stimulated and encouraged many children so that they decided on computing as a career path, an O- or even an A-level pass in the subject proved to be no guarantee of employment. The other brick thrown at the courses in the early 1980s came from higher education, which claimed that the courses did not provide appropriate preparation for degree work. Indeed, university lecturers claimed that they introduced bad habits, were teaching the children out-of-date information and that students with no background in the subject were preferable. Unfortunately, employers in major computing companies added that graduates from many universities had been taught out-of-date practices, were unaware of new developments and had been taught inappropriate languages.

So the place of computer studies in the curriculum is a difficult one. It is not in the core of the proposed national curriculum, nor is it considered to be an important option for the remainder. In some parts of the country it has been absorbed and redirected into another subject, information technology, which offers a broader base of knowledge although continuing to be centred around the microprocessor.

In the past it has proved to be a successful subject, with large numbers of children being entered for public examinations. For those with a dream of computing as a glamorous job, it brought a sense of reality, encouraging those who could respond and discouraging those who found the logic and problem analysis too difficult. Thus, for children who felt that computing offered an interesting career, it provided a testing ground to discover whether this was what they wished to do. Some took the exam and changed direction, while others found the stimulus to carry on further, appreciating that this was just the beginning. The core of computer studies revolves around problem solving and the development and use of rigorous logical thinking. While this is akin to mathematics, it has technical and applied elements that are very exciting to children with appropriate approaches and attitudes and are not found elsewhere in the curriculum. For them, self-confidence and a line of future activity emerge which would be missing if the subject disappeared.

Much of the early work in the subject involved the skills of programming, but selection of the languages that children learned has proved very debatable. Fortran and even Cobol were early contenders, and then interest swung to Basic although the advocates of Comal tried hard to prove that this was the better language. Pascal is now widely supported, but it is difficult as an entry language. Passing by has been Pilot and APL, while in the near future there is interest in a form of Prolog. The importance of 'C', particularly as the foundation of the operating system Unix, is unlikely to be reflected in its adoption as a language in courses for under 16s.

The question must be whether it matters. Fourth generation (and soon fifth generation) languages are increasingly the mainstay of professional work, and none of those taught in school will be used in general. Amateur or home microcomputer enthusiasts will continue to program, but they are largely self-taught and any school experience expands or underpins that learning. Behind the teaching of programming is the analysis of a problem, the creation of a logical structure and the use of a series of coding steps to achieve a possible solution. The learning attributes are the same, and it is the exercise of these that is important, not the syntax of the language itself. Useful also is the concept of the relationship between the language and the operating system.

In addition, the link to real-world applications is important. If the choice of the language is incidental, development of a conceptual understanding of the principle generic uses of the computer is significant. Through use in other subjects, most children will gain a practical knowledge of databases, wordprocessors, communications software, spreadsheets and so on, but there needs to be room for those with a particular interest in computer studies to explore and probe the concepts behind such programs. Structural analysis reveals much about the principles of approach and these are valuable in relating their use to resolving real-world problems.

It is through the links to problem analysis and logical structures that computer studies is educationally valuable, and the trend towards relating this to commercial and environmental applications enhances its place in the curriculum. Analyses of stock control, for example of shops, sporting equipment, varieties of plants in greenhouses, are obvious leads to databases and can be readily envisaged as having relevance to activities in the community. The work can be further enhanced by analysing related problems, introducing the use of bar code readers, security sensors and temperature/humidity control. Practical projects such as those that solve real problems give a sense of relevance to the work and at the same time develop understanding of the area of study and the concepts that underpin it.

While such examples are practical applications, they are not vocational in that they do not instantly lead to a career. Nevertheless, they do represent the degree to which a subject like this can support a vocational approach. Through such problem-solving exercises, there is much greater understanding of the applicability of the subject, its value and limitations within the confines of the technology and its acceptability within society. The debate on the absorption of facilities offered by the technology into society is one in which children need to develop their views and insight. By finding out why people hesitate or reject the new applications, and in particular the outcomes of their own projects, they become informed about the elements of a democratic debate – not just as a theoretical exercise but related to a personal involvement. This is a much richer experience, and gives a taste of the tensions and allegiances that emerge in such an argument.

The transience of the technology has forced teachers to consider the role of the subject in terms of principles and concepts rather than training in particular vocational skills. Associating these with projects and activities that are applicable within the community provides a sense of reality and purpose that offers more rewarding educational and social value than mere training. With the addition of debate over the social implications of the technology, children are better prepared for participating in their community and its discussions, as well as having knowledge that is useful in employment. It is this interpretation of the role of computer studies that seems to be prevailing in schools now.

Technology

This has become a much broader subject over the years. With its origins in a variety of sources, the old crafts of woodwork and metalwork, technical drawing, design technology, applied science, as well as the need to address the new developments, there is still a great deal of variation in approach and content. Here I am concerned only with the impact of microelectronics and information technology, but it is inevitable that some of the comments will refer to wider issues.

The attractions of technology for those concerned with an increase in vocational education are obvious, for the old crafts provided the foundation for many pupils who went on to be apprentices. In the days of technical schools, children learned carpentry, metalwork, welding, plastering and wallpapering, draughtsmanship, cooking, needlework, sewing, car maintenance and so on, all leading directly to immediate employment opportunities. However, these were all subjects taken by pupils with lesser academic ability. Those who were considered brighter were actively encouraged to avoid these subjects and aim for university where their future was considered better and the prestige of the school was enhanced. As someone who taught for many years in such a school, I am very aware of the pressure that I and my fellow teachers placed on the children.

The change over the last few years has been in the acceptance that technology is not just for the less able, but provides a valuable education for all children of both sexes. Unfortunately this is still not reflected in university entrance requirements, but the desperate search for children to study engineering subjects has reduced their entry levels. Until higher education begins to give greater status to qualifications in technology, the level of importance ascribed to the subject at school will not be raised.

The arrival of microelectronics as a technology that has so many applications in society has made it more important that children understand the principles that underline it. If we live in a society that depends on technology to control the environment, then it is essential that everybody understands, at least in general terms, how it works. Without such a background, sensible choices and arguments cannot be made when decisions are required, and this is already clear in the poor quality of understanding of civil servants and their views as adumbrated through government statements. Indeed, its importance is further shown in the helplessness and paralysis that occurs when there is a simple technical breakdown. When the machine stops, irritation rises through ignorance. Consider for example the behaviour and comments of those in trains and undergrounds when the system stops, in cars caught in a queue, at times of an electrical power cut, on receipt of an error in a computer bill, when the washing machine/video/microwave does not do what is wanted. How many times have we heard a mistake in social services payments blamed by government on 'computer error', although the same government spokespeople take all the credit when the computer despatches a bonus!

In November 1987, the European Parliament adopted a resolution underlining the importance of a *culture technologique* in the education of all young people. While this was aimed at the need for a large increase in the number of highly qualified engineers and also technicians to sustain our economic future, it also recognised that it was essential for *all* young people if our democracy was to continue in good health. The important word in this is 'all', for a grounding in the basic principles behind the technology should be part of everyone's education. Taught as a barren set of facts this will have little impact – nor will it motivate children to develop an initial interest in technology into a commitment to study it further.

Learning principles through practice is the cornerstone of good teaching in electronics. Many schools now use the 'Microelectronics for All' (MFA) kit as a broad introduction to the subject. Sometimes at primary or middle school, but more usually at secondary level, the kit encourages children to explore and experiment with a range of four input and four output devices. The target is first to establish the general principles of AND, OR and NOT, to add the facility of a counter module and, finally, the concepts behind memory. Additional outputs at this stage include the control of a buggy and the creation of simple tunes. In tackling this, children approach ideas through the need to solve simple but realistic problems: How is a light turned on when it is dark and off when it is light?; Design a doorbell for the deaf; How do you ensure that a machine is not switched on until the safety shield has been put in place? None of these are very difficult problems, but they stimulate discussion, trial and testing, analysis of the problem and thinking, planning and designing. On a small scale, this is the essence of the principles behind design and make that which is at the core of good technology education.

An alternative approach to microelectronics is component-centred. This requires children to learn about transistors, resistors, capacitors, etc, how they work and their properties. Small circuits are then established (for example on breadboards) and simple experiments are possible. This is the factual knowledge approach, where knowing about the devices is at least as important as creating a working model of some system. While children find activities with microelectronics stimulating because 'things work' quickly and simply, the component-centred approach does not easily introduce the essential problem-solving nature of technology. Having created circuits that resolve the issues as with MFA above, many children have the interest to wonder why they work like that and then study the components and how they operate. In this way motivation remains, and the children retain their appreciation of the practical relevance of what they are pursuing. For those who do not wish to examine the components in more detail, the exercises they have completed with the kit have helped them to achieve an understanding of some of the principles behind the technology and a general appreciation of how it works.

Of course this is only a small part of a possible course to develop such general understanding. Other elements should be added, but the approach is one that has proved very fruitful in stimulating interest and a broad perspective. This is a general introduction to technology, and from here any decision to take the subject further should result in a substantial proportion of work with electronics. Many kits providing the basis of experimental work have now been produced, and most are arranged to support a similar approach to that above – taking problems, analysing them, designing and creating a solution. From such a background, links to further education lead to further qualifications that have accepted vocational directions.

Courses such as these are not planned to produce immediate entry into related employment. The insight and skills developed are undoubtedly useful in a job, but to suggest that this is a directly vocational course is to misunderstand the generalised purpose of the background knowledge that is being learned. By approaching the subject in this way, children develop a broad range of concepts that they identify as relevant to the community in which they live. To believe that a child has acquired sufficient expertise to be more than an interested trainee in a suitable job overrates the depth that should be achieved. Other courses that ignore electronics but include the development of good problem-solving skills may be just as useful.

Creating circuits, installing components and hard programming controlling software can produce systems tailor-made for particular applications. None of this requires elaborate manufacturing machinery, and it is not difficult therefore to establish a garden shed industry to undertake this kind of work. Thus, children leaving school with appropriate knowledge could establish a small company to provide such a service. The school courses themselves are unlikely to provide sufficient background and detailed knowledge for this, but supplemented by suitable private study and courses at a college they could be sufficient to provide the knowledge to establish such a company. However, it could be argued justifiably that such tactics could be used to found similar working arrangements in jobs like hairdressing. The difference is that the development of microelectronic boxes is more demanding and commands a higher market price. Within this field, opportunities for company development are considerable although sustaining it has proved very difficult for many people in the last few years.

Controlling other devices

The essence of microelectronic boxes, as with so many applications of microelectronics, is control. Because this application is so widespread, control technology has become another potential avenue for vocational education. Indeed, the example of the particular garden shed industry referred to above is a potential outcome. Control is not, however, confined to microelectronics; much for example, is done with pneumatics, but it is the microelectronic side on which I want to concentrate here.

One of the main characteristics of mankind is the attempt to organise and control the environment. In both the agricultural and industrial ages there were elements of control: selecting, organising and timing the growth of plants and the domesticity of animals were hardly examples of chance; the development of machines to manufacture goods and transport them demonstrated a considerable degree of skill and management in harnessing the earth's resources to enhance and substitute for human energy and strength. However, the nature of control released by the power of the microprocessor refers to replacement and enhancement of activities that would normally be ascribed more to the brain than to the rest of the body.

To explain that, a few words about the behaviour of the brain may be helpful. Many activities of our body are automatic, for example temperature regulation, rate of the heart beat associated with exercise level, control of the hormone system, all organised in the brain through the hypothalamus. These are activities that would be expected in a well-designed engine or machine. Some bodily activities, such as the rate of breathing by the medulla, a system with which we can consciously interfere up to a point, are more deliberately controlled. Others become apparently automatic although they have been consciously learned and programmed, for example walking, riding a bicycle, processes often ascribed to the cerebellum. It is these activities which resemble those that the microprocessor now undertakes and are essential parts of our new ability to control our environment. The programming turns a complex series of interacting instructions into a controlled outcome. Walking is a very complex series of actions, yet most people do it with little conscious thought – even to the extent of avoiding pot-holes in the pavements without hesitating in a conversation or changing other activities that are taking place at the same time. Through the use of the microprocessor, similar controlled operations are now in widespread operation and can be seen in many factories or even in domestic machines.

The development of an increasing quantity of such control devices is a part of current technical progress. Understanding the principles by which they work introduces the concepts behind monitoring, analysis, problem solving and feedback. Through illustrations of relevant applications, pupils gain an appreciation of the technological approach to meeting humanity's ambition to control its environment, and this can be reinforced by children preparing simulated examples or at least simple programs to operate them.

Much has already been established to support this. Many primary schools make use of programmable toys such as Big Track so that children develop an understanding of the procedure of forecasting a control sequence, monitoring and where necessary amending it. Further work with turtles and the language Logo leads to insights into control although that is not necessarily the intention. By preparing short programs, the children are able to create shapes on the screen as well as directing the turtle to repeat them by drawing on paper. Again, errors or improvements can be identified and the program rewritten to attempt to achieve the desired result. The turtle is under the control of the program, which the children are writing and amending.

In further work with Logo in primary schools, children have been encouraged to control a variety of devices. For example, whole arrays of fairground sideshows have been created in LEGO bricks and then operated. In undertaking this kind of work the feedback from the system has been largely that observed by the children, but in most practical uses of control technology the feedback is provided by sensors that are built into the system. This increases the complexity, but is easy for children to appreciate from such a background.

Kits are being used in schools of all levels to explore this. Technical LEGO has proved very popular, and with one set children are able to create a wide range of miniature machines: for example conveyor belts, lifts, arms, and buggies. Sensors are built into some of them and can be wired to the control box which itself may be connected to a computer running a simple and self-explanatory control program. Thus, it is possible to simulate the process of planning and designing a machine, monitoring its performance, preparing a control program, establishing it as if it was built into the system and observing the results.

To approach the activities, children are presented with realistic problems to solve; to design an automatic barrier for a multi-storey car park; to design a device that will sort two different sized blocks and direct them to different bins; or to design a sliding door mechanism for a supermarket. None requires much technical knowledge, and nearly all children find it very easy to build things with LEGO bricks. What is required is logical analysis of the problem and a structured approach to solving it.

To provide teachers with an insight into what they hoped would be achieved, the designers of the kit produced the following list of skills and attitudes that they expected would result from this work.

The ability to analyse a problem.
The ability to search for information.

The ability to formulate ideas for solutions.
The ability to evaluate ideas against criteria and select the best.
The ability to develop ideas into a working model and a software program.
The ability to evaluate a solution against set criteria.
The ability to communicate effectively using whatever means is most appropriate.

Problem solving can be enjoyable and successful. Co-operation can lead to more effective problem solving. (Tecmedia, 1986)

These skills and attitudes are the same as would be expected from most work with technology using this exploratory and problem-oriented approach. The LEGO kits are particularly successful in stimulating this, but others that use the same style would lead to similar learning experiences.

There was much interest in the early 1980s in the use of robot arms. Increasingly important in manufacturing industry, their control by the microcomputer seemed an interesting simulation of the real world. A number were produced, some very elaborate and made with considerable sophistication giving as many as five or six points of rotation. The software to program the arms was not too difficult to write, but the activities that children found to do with them were very limited. Once they had used them to pick up an object and move it to another place, the interest was gone. However, when the arm is used as part of the solution to a problem, as for example picking specific items from a conveyor belt, then it becomes a useful and realistic part of the simulation of control that is being explored. As a tool on its own its interest value and stimulus to learning is limited, but as part of the solution to a problem it becomes a necessary device that provokes investigation of its capability and control.

Work to the level that has been described so far is within the capacity of all children, and for many it stimulates further investigation and deeper understanding. However, even those with no bent towards technology gain from experience in the activities referred to above as they have more understanding of the mechanisms that are managing the environment in which they live. While the details are not important, they are aware that automatic doors require sensors to see them coming, timing to open so that they are not stopped in their normal progress, a sensor to notice they have passed through so that the doors can close again, and a simple program to regulate the interaction between the pieces of information that are received. There is no magic, no spy on their privacy (although they will be aware that this could be incorporated), no human intervention. If there is a stoppage, they have sufficient insight to appreciate a range of places where a breakdown could have occurred. They can begin to think systematically and logically even if they have no idea of how a transistor works or even what one looks like. The processes of the experience of establishing solutions to problems through control have expanded the range of procedures they have available to deal with events that they meet in life.

For some children, the interest in control will develop into a desire for further experience and study. This may form part of computer studies or design and technology, or be a special area on its own. The links to the other two subjects are clear from what has been written in earlier paragraphs, and the treatment is in the same style. However, many other subjects can benefit from work in control technology. Monitoring rainfall and temperature can be used as sensors to regulate the opening and closing of greenhouses or the supply of water to animals. In many experiments in physics, the use of control can lead to more precise measurements. In geography, physical education, drama – indeed in most disciplines – it is not difficult to conceive of points at which the use of this technology would enhance the work being done. Using these occasions not only presents those studying the technology with real problems to solve, it also demonstrates to those learning the particular subject how widely it is used to help man to control his environment.

Working on projects that reflect real-world situations gives a sense of purpose to the studies. Many schools are now introducing computer-assisted design activities, perhaps linked to a simulation of computer-aided manufacture (CADCAM), an application widely advocated for industry although still too infrequently used. In its most simple form, this will produce outputs of designs on plotters, perhaps using digitisers or video images as part of the inputs. All these are techniques used in industry, sometimes with no greater level of sophistication than that available in schools. The key to successful learning, however, rests with links to realistic and relevant problems to solve or simulations of real-world situations to explore.

Control technology is not itself a vocational subject, but those who have developed an understanding of its approach and techniques have acquired fundamental concepts for moving into fields of engineering. Based on the systems approach, dependent on feedback, it is at the hub of the application of scientific principles in the resolution of problems that help mankind to control the environment. Nobody is a 'trained control technologist' yet (and I rather hope never will be) but everybody, either at the level of appreciating what is happening or at the more practical level of creating solutions, will be meeting its applications and should have explored and experienced it.

Business and commerce

In theory, this subject seems totally vocational in orientation. Children who have studied secretarial courses at school in the past have often gone straight into commercial employment. Some have spent a short period at college obtaining RSA qualifications, while others have taken them part-time while doing junior office jobs. From some schools, it has been possible to take the RSA qualifications as part of the course. Thus the tradition of the subject has been oriented very much towards jobs and a vocational application.

With the appearance of information technology, the same direction has been maintained although the typewriter has gradually been replaced by the wordprocessor on the microcomputer. Although offices have taken some time to make such changes, most have now replaced their typewriters at least for an electronic device even if they have not actually managed to invest in a computer. The changes have been as slow and difficult for them as it has been for schools to make the required investment in equipment.

Information technology, however, is much more than a wordprocessor. While this may be the centre of the typist's desk, often the filing is now in an electronic database, the accounts on a spreadsheet, the presentation prepared through a graph plotter, and the office messages transmitted by electronic mail. Perhaps 'often' is an exaggeration for several of these systems, but progress towards this type of régime is taking place. Although I have listed them as separate pieces of software, in practice many will be linked and the future will undoubtedly see total integration. For many secretaries, their role will continue to change as their employers begin to use their own terminals for an increasing amount of correspondence, but the churning out of standard letters and contracts on the wordprocessor will continue for many years. In the meantime, however, there is still a demand for dictation and even audio-typing, the production of memos, the days of filing, and the ledger for petty cash and postage stamps.

Any response from education has to take account of this mixture of old and new practices, and also of the variety of new work that is beginning to appear. With the appearance of desk-top publishing, small home-based businesses are appearing which exploit this technology profitably. There is a need, for example, for leaflets, club notices and small posters, which can be readily produced by this method. As the quality of laser printers improves, in particular with the addition of colour, there will be a substantial number of such ventures.

Just as these are likely to be based in a domestic environment, so will other secretarial practices. Electronic communication methods make the place of work, certainly the office, subject to much more variation. Managers as much as secretaries can operate from such a base. If such practices become common, there are a number of personal adjustments and attitude changes that have to be developed. These people are likely to be self-employed, as will most people if Barry Pitson's play 'Tickets for the Titanic: Everyone's a Winner', on Channel 4 is to be believed, and that raises its own financial problems.

To produce a course of vocational training for such a wide range of needs is therefore difficult. If training in particular software, on particular machines, or in certain skills such as shorthand is provided, for many children it will prove irrelevant and may even be a disadvantage. The machines are changing, and the current Amstrads, Apples and IBMs will be replaced, probably at first by more integrated equipment. Input systems such as keyboards will change, even if the principles remain the same. There is no international standard for the layout of a keyboard, and different equipment will give different names to some of the keys. The variety of software that is already available for such fundamental activities as wordprocessing is a small indication of the many changes and differences that will continue to occur. Many people were training on the early versions of Wordstar with its long list of control-(*) commands to organise its facilities. This was quite a learning exercise if one did not want to look up every command to be used each time but happily, with the arrival of WIMP environments, all that is now defunct and can be forgotten. Anybody who learned them can forget them, unless their office or equipment has not yet changed to more modern software. Yet how many schools are still teaching children these codes? Teachers have told me proudly that they train their children on Wordstar, and I am not aware that they have stopped yet. Other teachers have said they have bought Amstrads or IBMs as these are machines that the children will find in the offices they will join. However, will they still be there when the children arrive? If so, for how much longer? Training to that level of detail in a rapidly changing technology is bound to lead to the acquisition of totally irrelevant knowledge.

For schools then, the aim has to be concepts and principles, exploring facilities and their functions rather than learning the details of a particular system. Use leads to understanding and children need to experience basic generic software such as wordprocessors, but that use should be in the context of meeting particular needs rather than as an isolated exercise. Nobody has yet produced the perfect wordprocessor, and indeed the nature of that perfection will change with more experience and the definition of more facilities. However, it is still possible to outline the principle characteristics that can be expected from such software and appreciate the range of opportunities that could be available. The way in which the program is organised on the screen, the methods adopted for accessing and using the various features, will naturally vary between manufacturers but the principles will be the same. The same can be said for most other types of generic software.

So even here, where the connections with vocational education are most obvious, the new technology has introduced so much uncertainty that it is quite inappropriate to consider the role of the subject to be that of particular training. Yet again, the most appropriate activities for school are to provide children with a broad learning experience, preferably tied to practical applications.

The Hampshire Business and Information Studies Project is a good example of the approach that is needed. Included is considerable use of wordprocessing, spreadsheets, databases, and even communication systems, but these are not the purpose of the courses. Instead they are used as natural tools that are needed in an active office environment, and are learned at the time and to the degree which is needed for the current activity. Opportunities for taking a particular technical study further are usually available, but the aim is to use the programs to support the work rather than be a study in themselves.

For the real motivating force, the children are involved in simulations of office and business activity. They undertake market research; visit real offices and businesses to interview people; set up mini-companies; and process, file and maintain records and transactions, usually working in teams with individuals who are assigned specific responsibilities. The whole is a carefully planned and integrated set of assignments and projects that develop such skills as information management and decision making in a relevant setting, and encourage such attitudes as co-operation and personal/social interaction. The atmosphere of classes working well in this way is one of excitement, purposefulness and creativity, not of passive absorption.

Just as in the real-world office, the technology has provided a set of tools that can reduce the chores of the work, improve the quality of presentation and speed up the processing of data, information and organisation. If the technology was not available, such projects would have required so much time for dealing with the material that was collected that there would have been too little left to develop the useful learning and performance skills. The value of the technology for the office may need pointing out, but its advantages for children's activities are apparent. Facilities that are useful clearly emerge from the work, and may even be suggested to some of the offices which are visited or at which work experience is undertaken.

Old skills such as shorthand still have their value in certain commercial environments, and also for such jobs as journalism for example. However, the dominant feature of the business and office environment now is the technology, and courses that fail to spend a substantial proportion of their time helping children to appreciate the facilities this provides and then understand the concepts behind them, preferably in a practical way, are not helping them to prepare for the environment in which they will live and work. Training in a particular piece of software or even in shorthand should be a post-school activity when the relevance and need is clearly identified, not expected of everybody when for most it will become redundant knowledge.

Conclusion

Learning about the equipment, the technology, computing and even business studies all seem useful areas for training for vocational applications. Indeed, they reflect areas where there is likely to be a substantial demand for employees for many years to come. If training is limited to familiarity and an understanding of the concepts and facilities behind these new developments, then school provides an important arena in which these can be explored and appreciated. On the other hand, another definition of training is to develop specific skills in the use of a technology or piece of software, and it is clear that these would be entirely inappropriate activities for schools.

By learning through the practical approaches outlined above, children learn to put the significance and value of the technology in its appropriate place. Understanding of particular features, properties and techniques emerges because the relevance and necessity for them is seen as assisting them in meeting certain situations or needs. Sometimes these may require pointing out by teachers, but they are met incidentally and remembered because they are associated with specific activities and projects.

Of equal importance is the value of these approaches in helping children to develop skills and attitudes that have universal value. Problem solving, decision making, design and make strategies, all arise naturally through these approaches to the technology and its applications. Helping to ensure they are transferable between subjects is a much bigger challenge.

References

Tecmedia (1986) *Teachers Materials* Technic LEGO 1455, Loughborough

Chapter 2

The Accessibility of Information

Introduction

In spite of the diversity of their applications, the appearance of microprocessors has introduced significant effects in only three main areas: the control of the environment, some aspects of which were discussed in the last chapter; obtaining, storing and managing information; and a widespread accessibility to information brought about by an increasing range of mechanisms for communication. It is with the last two areas that this chapter is concerned.

The difficulty with the word 'information' is that it has many different meanings. In this chapter, I want to deal only with information as recorded data or facts – those which provide the raw material and evidence for learning. Other uses of the word, for example the information that comes from recording experimental results, will be covered later.

Most of the examples used will refer to written information, which is for convenience and because it forms the bulk of that which is currently used in schools. The situation is changing, for example with the greater availability of video recorders, and increasingly the importance of visual information is being recognised. However, the present state of technology still makes it relatively hard for teachers and children to manipulate and organise stores of visual information, although this will become easier in the future. Nonetheless, it is worth recognising that a substantial majority of people gain most of their knowledge from visual information sources, and that educationists, because of the difficulties of handling them, have generally neglected to use such sources effectively up to the present time.

Forms of information storage

Before discussing the impact that the new information systems have on learning, a superficial description of the range of forms of storage will provide a suitable background. Many are still not widely available in schools, and some present difficult organisational problems for teachers and in particular for funding and resources. Some indication of these will be given in this section and later. Also, just as the technology and software is developing, so too is the means of access to much of the information; this should therefore not be regarded as a static area.

Information stores can be conveniently divided into local and remote. The former are usually held in the institution, indeed generally attached to the particular computer that the child or teacher is using. Remote stores are obviously held some distance away, often in different countries, and these will be described later.

The most obvious form of local information store is the database on a floppy disc that the school itself has created or that has been bought. Such stores may contain, for example, information that children in a class have themselves collected and use to learn about numbers, graphs or just their own behaviour; information collected on a field trip about the wildlife; information gleaned from census returns about the area in which they live; information about entries into external examinations; or the personal profiles of individual children being used for assessment. The size of the database is governed by the capacity of the disc or discs, and it is accessed by means of the same program that was used when it was stored. Some schools may keep such information available on a network, although the last two items are of such a confidential nature that the discs would normally be retained in a secure place.

These are databases for limited internal use. Now that hard discs have become very much cheaper, it is possible to make them much larger and still access at reasonable speed the information they contain. This could mean that they contain several megabytes of data, but in most school uses they are likely to be very much smaller.

In terms of size, a database stored on a CD Rom could be very much larger. The CD Rom has been developed using the same production technology as that used for CD music discs, and is read in the same way by a laser. Its current storage capacity is about 550 megabytes – the equivalent of something like 150,000 printed pages. That is substantial, and it is not surprising that the first discs that have been produced have much unused space! While these are for purchase, users are not able to prepare their own databases on such discs. Other members of this CD family are arriving which carry sound and pictures as well as textual information. The problem is that sound and, in particular, pictures require a substantial storage space, so the total capacity of material on the discs drops considerably.

Video is more widely recognised under the titles of videodisc and interactive video. Similar technology is involved – that is, the use of lasers for reading the information – but the diameter of the disc is twelve inches. The capacity is 54,000 still pictures per side, which is also considerable. If these are run as a movie at 25 frames a second, then they would last just over half an hour. The pictures could be replaced by writing, or such text could be inserted like teletext in the interframe space and recalled in the same way as Ceefax or Oracle. Naturally sound can accompany the pictures, two separate channels being available so that different languages could be offered. All these separate pictures or frames of text are individually identifiable, and thus addressable and quickly accessible. Therefore this is a database, principally of visual information.

Those are the major forms of local databases, all able to be linked to the microcomputer, some having to be purchased, others creatable by the user and all able to be manipulated to varying degrees. The range of these will grow and develop over time, but there must be a question mark over whether the user needs all the information close at hand like this or finds it more economic to access a remote database to obtain answers.

There are two sorts of remote database; on-line and broadcast. While the former are probably the best known in education, the use of the latter will develop as the facilities and extent of the subject matter increases. On-line means connection between the computer and the machine holding the database through a direct link, and this usually involves the telephone. In practice, such a connection requires a modem. Progress towards cabling cities and, later, the rest of the country is slow, but when it has occurred connections to remote databases will be able to take place faster. Cabling differs from telephone lines in that it supports the transmission of a much wider range of signals, including television, and therefore the speed and versatility of links to remote databases will be much improved. Whether all the country will ever be cabled has to be questioned, for it is clearly uneconomic to lay these to the remoter rural areas. However, maintaining cohesion within society requires that if parts of the country are cabled then the rest should also be, even if that is at a financial loss.

The range of remote on-line databases is growing constantly. To join them, the majority require some form of membership (usually at a price) to receive a password to provide access to the material. Some make no further charges, whereas others require payment for the pages accessed, the time connected, or the type of enquiry. To search a database the user works with the commands it provides, and the user's own microcomputer is merely a dumb terminal to it. However, information from the database can be downloaded into the microcomputer and manipulated by any suitable software that the user has. Thus, quotations from a remote database can be inserted into an article that the user is preparing with his or her wordprocessor.

There are hundreds of these databases available now, covering a very wide range of topics. Some are very specialised, dealing for example with law, glass technology, financial information, industrial hazards in the chemical industry, or a bibliography of books. Because many have been developed for specific industrial groups, access to them may be restricted. Some are more general, such as World Reporter which carries the full text of selected newspapers and broadcasts from around the world; others such as Prestel carry general information grouped into particular categories, including complete computer programs, In education, NERIS provides bibliographical reference to much material available to schools as well as the full text of some items. The significance of these databases is growing steadily, and items from World Reporter and the major American database, The Source, are quoted now as authoritative references in other publications.

Databases are also available on the electronic mail service targeted on education, The Times Network for Schools (TTNS). Some of these have been developed on a national basis to be available to all users, while others have been created for specific local education authorities by their own staff and offer only limited access. Other uses of electronic mail will be referred to later.

One important aspect of the on-line database is the ability to probe it for the information required. Different services require their own sets of commands for this procedure, but the system works on the interaction of the user with the database. The broadcast system of remote databases does not provide that facility, as the user merely receives the total database and employs local software or a previously received program to probe and manipulate it.

In their public form, broadcast databases are the Ceefax and Oracle teletext services of the BBC and IBA. Transmission is alongside pictorial information using some of the lines between the individual frames. Other countries offer their own teletext services, and similar transmissions could be provided via satellite to any part of the world. No one needs to connect with the computer, and all within the footprint of the broadcast can receive the data provided they have the appropriate equipment. For public transmissions, no fees are charged and no password is necessary.

The teletext services offer only a limited database for the general public, although they do include some software that schools may find useful. However, there is also a Datacast service which provides much larger databases, and which has the potential to supply substantial quantities of information. Receiving equipment is usually left switched on and coded to accept only those data items required. Charging systems can be built into the receiving equipment should that be desirable. The Datacast services are currently limited to particular clients and make use of only a few transmission lines. ECCTIS, which helps children to select their University by providing information about places available, supplies the general information using a CD Rom. In the hectic month of August, when the information is changing daily if not hourly, such a system is impractical. Updates are therefore transmitted by Datacast, and schools can capture this and run it alongside the CD Rom program.

Weather, news, financial and betting information are other examples of Datacast services, but the full potential of this substantial updating service has still to be developed.

Those are the forms of database that are available. Accessing by children is not always straightforward. Naturally there should be no problems with local databases, although guidelines on the methods of searching them may need to be available. Trusting children with CD Rom and interactive video equipment should not raise difficulties. However, the use of remote on-line databases raises other isues.

These databases usually require passwords, which should be considered to be precious and confidential pieces of information, as are those for personal mail boxes. To avoid having to share this widely, a possible solution is to ensure that access is limited to the use of a particular modem by introducing a unique signal from that device as part of the connection sequence. This then provides the opportunity for 'licensing' certain modems for connection to the database, and it then does not matter which phone or computer is used to act with the link. Teachers wishing to work from home merely take with them one of these modems. Children can have access provided they are using the identified devices.

Another issue is cost. There are two elements to this: the fees charged by the database itself, whatever the mechanism used, and the time cost while using the telephone line. By using the Packet Switched Service or Multistream, time on the line is usually charged only at local call rates, but complex searches can make these costs significant. Various mechanisms can be used by schools to manage these uses: permission for certain children only; access through only one system (for example that in the library) with supervision to hand; or a monitoring program on the computer although this is unlikely to be able to record the database charges on every system. The least satisfactory system from the educational viewpoint is that all searches should be conducted by or through a teacher. Learning to search and retrieve information through such databases is important as these will be major tools in the pupils' future. Schools need to address issues like those above, budget for the costs involved, and accept that the telephone is a significant expenditure centre in its educational activity.

Learning to use information

One of the difficulties with this subject is the confusion of words. In common with a number of other people, I use the word 'data' to describe the raw material; when order and organisation has been given to data, it becomes information; process this information with strategies and conceptual thinking, and hopefully that becomes knowledge. The trouble is that one person's knowledge is another's information, and most recorded information becomes the data for new research and development. That is confusing! It is always helpful to categorise things so that they can be given order and fitted into a pattern, but these words – data, information and knowledge – have meaning relative only to the user of the material, not the items themselves. What is knowledge to teachers, having been carefully thought through and understood by them, may be one piece of the information that children use to create their own insight.

Much has been written in recent years about the need for children to acquire information skills. Again, there has been some confusion about what this means. For many who fuse information skills with 'learning to learn', these are the various methods necessary to identify what is needed, and then locate and retrieve the information being sought. Naturally, these are important and necessary skills but they only touch the surface of the issues involved in using information. To be useful, the items retrieved have to be analysed, synthesised and evaluated as well – in other words used creatively in order to establish knowledge. Because that is really what all learning is about, these extra stages have often been assumed to be present. Maybe for many teachers that is true, but for a significant number of pupils and in much of the writing about information handling these are the neglected stages.

It has always seemed surprising that information handling and use has not assumed a much higher level of importance in education. Perhaps this is because we have generally taken it for granted, and believed that learning 'just happens'. Fundamentally, learning or acquiring knowledge is concerned with the business of processing information, but that does mean getting hold of it and using it creatively. Probably the best known guide to this is the Schools Council Curriculum Bulletin, *Information Skills in the Secondary Curriculum*. (Marland, 1981). Whether it would have been so well known had it not been issued free to every secondary school is debatable, for important as the subject is, it receives very little priority in educational concerns.

In his book, Marland identifies nine questions or stages in order to handle information effectively. These are:

1. What do I need to do?
2. Where could I go?
3. How do I get to the information?
4. Which resources shall I use?
5. How shall I use the resources?
6. What should I make a record of?
7. Have I got the information I need?
8. How should I present it?
9. What have I achieved?

Starting from deciding what the subject matter is, the procedure ends with an evaluation of whether what has been collected answers the questions. This, however, is about information skills, not the use of the results. While that is our main concern, the arrival of the technology has had a significant effect on information skills and it is useful to review this first.

Much work is done traditionally in primary education to collect and sort data. Beginning with a study of the characteristics of children in a classroom, it evolves into collecting data on, for example, wildlife in the vicinity of the school, the environment of shops and similar features, the traffic, food, and other topics that arise naturally from the projects in which children are involved. Before the technology, the data was collated by the children on paper and then presented for discussion on bar graphs and other forms of display. The patterns, thus formed gave the background to a developing understanding of the organisation of data into information that could be used to elucidate ideas and draw conclusions. While these words were not necessarily used, most children gathered that creating the patterns made it easier to deal with the data, and then they could arrive at interesting statements about, for example, the average height of the class or the most numerous species of bird in the area.

Working this way took up much time, and although many children were involved in the calculations and therefore became conscious of what was being done, the actual processes of producing the displays became an end in themselves and the interest in the information that emerged was reduced. Using simple databases to do the same job teaches not only how such software works as there is a need to define fields and arrange the screen display of each record, but also is much faster and maintains interest in the actual research. The collection of the data is still undertaken manually, although at a later age children will use the technology to do some of this too – for example recording the weather or counting the traffic.

Starting from the position of collecting data and filling the results into the program gives a clearer sense of how the information is generated from such a collation. Children can appreciate the inaccuracies, assumptions that are made, and the analysis that is often necessary to place some things into categories that do not obviously belong to them. In other words, the mystique of a database is shaken by the errors and warts that the children see being placed in it. For many this will not be obvious, and part of the teacher's role must be to draw out and establish in children's minds a scepticism and questioning attitude to the validity and reliability of information in whatever form it is provided.

Having gone through the process of creating a database, children should now be encouraged to search others for information. The variety available has already been described and all should be open to exploration for information, initially under the guidance and encouragement of teachers but later at the initiative of the children themselves. Some should be used to identify lists of references to other sources of data and information; such lists should include artefacts and people as well as texts and audio-visual resources. As the children become more experienced, the use of full text databases should be encouraged, searching by selecting keywords to identify pieces of relevant writing that can be downloaded as quotable sections or as the whole original.

Just as the creation of databases is learned through the need to organise data into a form that can be handled (in other words, in the activities associated with solving a problem), so the use of the range of databases suggested above is most opportunely undertaken in the context of needing to search and find out some information for a purpose. Lessons on 'database techniques' for the non-computer specialist are not necessary unless they relate to a particular need. Naturally, it is useful to review the types of facilities available, the methods of accessing any database of resources and where support and guidance from human assistants can be obtained, but learning how to handle different systems should be done only when it is needed.

Nearly all subjects at all levels are studied with an increasing emphasis on assignments and projects. Problems are set to be explored and knowledge is developed from the information that is identified and processed. In doing this work, children are involved in obtaining data, and organising information into patterns which they can then begin to understand. If much of this searching is not done through a variety of electronic databases, they are not preparing themselves for the real world in which they are going to live. The old solution to a 'project' was to find the entry in an encyclopedia, the more intelligent children copying it out in their own words, the less bright using the actual form of the entry. Regrettably, the information rarely passed through their conscious mind at all. Part of the reason for this was the difficulty of finding other sources of information, but this should no longer be such a problem. Unfortunately most texts are still paper-based and searching them is a time-consuming exercise, but as more become available as part of an electronic store, so it will be possible to use keywords to find the relevant entry for quotation or study.

The 'learning to learn' movement is now persistent, and very relevant to future needs. While there is an argument for its occurrence at the beginning of a course, it is always introduced in the arid 'this is what you will need' approach. Much more useful is its appearance when there are appropriate course activities that need to be undertaken. This is particularly true of information skills, for they are soon forgotten if they are not exercised with a purpose in mind, a problem to solve. There is also considerable value in reviewing the techniques that have been used at the end of a course, as they then form a background for learning that will continue in a different context or with other teachers. Transfer of skills such as these are notoriously difficult, as they are rightly considered in the context of the problem and approach that a particular subject demands. Using 'Chemical Abstracts' for finding sources of information for chemistry is quickly appreciated, but the same student frequently needs encouragement to use 'Social Science Abstracts' on a course that benefits from them. Put like this it sounds obvious, but in practice the approaches to the subject are different and the mental link does not necessarily occur. If the strategies for storing information are generalised from specific experiences that students have had, the transfer becomes easier.

The procedures of the Marland strategy listed above are fundamental to the process of obtaining information, even if that data is stored electronically or optically using one of the systems mentioned in the previous section. The appearance of the technology has made data more accessible, and this means that information skills should become more important in education. While there are some mechanical actions to be taken to obtain data from the system, they are not difficult to acquire and recall if the principles are introduced early in primary school and developed with practical applications at secondary level.

In some ways, the technology has helped to bring information closer to the student. Its accessibility through the system is one factor, but its presentation and legibility have also been made more approachable. Many old records, for example, were difficult to read, carefully stored for preservation, and often confusing to correlate. Recorded in a database, the information is legible and much easier for children to use. The links between maps that are artificially divided into pages in printed documents show their interrelationships more clearly scrolling on a screen or as apparently continuous film. Using a relational database, interconnections between different lists of scientific data can help to create understanding where previously a great deal of page turning and cross-referencing would have been needed.

Just as there has been great authority given to information in newspapers or by the BBC, so there has been a tendency to suggest that a computer never lies, and the information it contains must be true. No computer has that much authority, of course, for each is subject to the selectivity of what and how the information has been 'entered' for conveyance through the different carriers, be it the paper, the broadcast or the print-out. Primary sources of information are always given more credence than secondary, and that is generally justified. In most cases electronic and optical stores are used as secondary sources, although there are important exceptions to this. For example, such stores are used as more permanent methods of keeping old records, sometimes as photographs on discs, sometimes re-entered. Current data are often put into such databases first so that they become the primary source, and this applies not only to such records as births, marriages and deaths, but also to texts of publications. Increasingly, electronic and optical stores of information will become the first point of call to search for data and references, but it is important that children and students recognise the level of source with which they are dealing. Provided the entry is accurate, the records will be as authoritative as from any other source. While primary sources are rightly those to which students should usually turn if they are able, they too can be as fallible as the romantic memories of the days of steam in the mind of the old engine driver.

Whatever the source, information has to be treated sceptically, looking for bias and errors. When Crick and Watson (Watson, 1968) were searching for the structure of DNA, they were frustrated by the shape of the bases - the 'building blocks'. Having checked them in various reference books, they found that they would not fit the helix they had created. Then a colleague pointed out that the shape Crick and Watson were using was wrong, and that different reference books had perpetuated the mistake by copying the first erroneous drawing. Of course, the right shape fitted the spiral perfectly. Testing the validity of information and being sceptical about the authority of sources is an important element of all searches and work on assignments and projects.

A now famous exercise for children, developed for MEP by Ann Irving (Irving and Gawith, 1984) and her colleagues, required children in different groups to play the roles of journalists preparing a story. One group used a wordprocessor for the piece in a newspaper, one for a radio news broadcast, and another for a teletext page. Information for the story came over news agency tapes, simulated by another computer and adding further details as they became available, so it was constantly changed and updated. The constraints were time and space - both realistic problems for journalists. From this very successful exercise, many educational lessons were learned. One of the most significant was the introduction of the children to the partiality, bias and often unintentional inferences that emerge in a story and colour their interpretation of it. The problem of one side's freedom fighter being the other side's terrorist became very real. For how long their scepticism of the authority and validity of reports by these media was maintained is not known, but such an exercise is important in helping children to appreciate that interpreted information is not always as accurate as they unconsciously assume.

Another problem that arises is understanding the information that children receive. In *Knowledge, Information Skills and the Curriculum*, David Hopkins (1987) reports on research done on mathematical worksheets for some widely used school schemes. It was clear that in several instances the children failed to do the mathematics because they did not understand the information. Indeed, in some of the examples given it was very difficult to obtain an accurate comprehension of both the data given and the conclusion for which the question was searching. When tackling a series of problems, children (and adults as well) go into automatic procedures if they possibly can. By learning the teacher's body language, the arrangement of the text, the organisation of the blackboard example, children become 'curriculum-wise' (a term Hopkins uses, which seems very appropriate) and deal with difficulties or problems in as repetitious a manner as possible. Regrettably such clues are not usually around in the real world or even in the next classroom, and so transfer from the apparent learning experience does not take place. However, if the problem is presented in the same way in the examination paper, such children will secure high marks!

Using databases has to be easy for the child to find them valuable. Problems must not arise in understanding how to use them, though misunderstanding the information that is received at the end of a search is a hazard for which the system is not responsible. Early databases created difficulties for children in understanding the search procedure. When they had mastered it the procedure became automatic or, put another way, the children had become 'database-wise'. Unfortunately, they had not learned *how* their approach worked, and therefore had to start at the beginning when they operated another system. Information at the front end, the way into the system, needs to be totally obvious for children to be able to appreciate the principles and transfer their skills to other databases.

Learning to use information must not be restrained or inhibited by the complexity of the system. Techniques learned for one system should provide sufficient principles to enable children to transfer and use different ones without difficulty. As most systems are now dependent on a form of keyword searching procedure, some difficulties of the past seem to be disappearing. Keywords bring useful analytical benefits with them also. The process of identifying the appropriate words to start the search, to link with others and to replace with synonyms or related words, requires a careful dissection of the issues for which information is required and some thoughtful identification of the salient features of the work being done. Any assignment or project work needs this type of thinking, but it is necessary when using a database in order to achieve any level of success.

Emerging from such a search should be a range of possible sources of information, and the next useful exercise is the process of selecting the valuable and relevant ones and discarding the others. While it is possible to use just one entry, it is often difficult to identify which is the single source to choose. Thus the disciplines of analysis and selection that an electronic database carries with it introduce useful educational benefits of their own.

Some people regret the loss of serendipity that comes from using a good database. While there is some truth in this, a new practice, which can be called a form of serendipity, has emerged instead. Because a good database will give a range of 'hits' from a search, there is an opportunity to follow up unwanted ones if the context or title is interesting. There may not be any aimless but interesting page flipping that characterises much current serendipitous experiences, but the results are not dissimilar. A fast forward run through a videotape or even a videodisc can lead to a number of side-tracks that provoke interesting discoveries. An electronic or optical database may seem hidden and straightjacketed on the surface, but playing with it - using strange combinations of keywords, flicking between pictures - can lead to new experiences that can enrich the user.

The value of serendipity is the potential for exciting a new interest or generating some fresh insight from a combination of events. Within a society that is obviously suffering from information overload, it would be natural to conclude that the development of personal interests would arise readily and spontaneously. Yet, for that to happen, children need to develop the background and enthusiasm to create interests of their own through their education.

Forcing a particular interest on a child is counter-productive, and it would be totally erroneous to suggest that interests have to be academic or intellectual to be acceptable. However, there are many people who could benefit and develop their personalities and abilities from interests and who fail to recognise and follow one. Economically, there is potential for progress, since many new ideas, inventions and businesses emerge from an interest that evolves into a mainstream activity or career. The present world of information technology and computer businesses is littered with people who have once been enthusiasts and now find it their main line of work.

Successful development of an interest is concerned with fostering and responding to natural curiosity, and encouraging enthusiasm. With the appearance of the new technologies, and in particular databases, the possibility of uncovering information that underpins an interest and then exploring connections is greatly enhanced. As the storage and accessibility increases, so the potential for uncovering new aspects grows, but children need to be aware of how to go about this, how to spot the new avenue that can be pursued, and how to get further help without embarrassment or discomfort.

This information can be obtained on a worldwide basis through the interconnections of the new communication systems. An interest that is not shared is not supported and encouraged, and these same communication systems can help to create links with people, some of whom may be living at considerable distances from each other. The more esoteric and unusual the interest, the more likely this is. Through the new technologies, the opportunities for expanding, discussing and developing an interest have been much increased, but they will not be used unless education helps children to recognise the directions of their curiosity and accept that there is ready access to facilities which will help them to satisfy it.

Communications

The development and sharing of interests gain a great deal from the way in which the technology has helped to improve and extend the range of communication systems that are available. Much comment is made about the information explosion, but this is made more apparent and an issue by the communication systems explosion that has accompanied it. Not only is there more information available, but its arrival in homes and offices is also more rapid and through a wider variety of systems. Transmitting information has moved from drawing in the sand and tribal parleys of the folk-lore of the community to cable and satellite, which bring all parts of the world closer together. Imprecision in transmission has been much reduced, from the time when the elders passed on the traditions of the group to the young men through increasingly distorted stories, to the present use of very accurate digital codes.

Through the use of these technologies the world seems to be getting smaller. Events from every country are presented through the television set or arrive through the telephone line almost as soon as they happen. To such an extent has this occurred that one is now critical if there are no immediate pictures of an event that is taking place or being described. The perception of the world is that it is close at hand through the medium of the screen. If it cannot be visited physically, if everybody cannot be everywhere at the same time, then at least the experiences can be sampled second hand and, more importantly, the attitudes, approaches and responses of people in other lands can be heard and perhaps understood.

Although the television set is the focus of so much of this information explosion, paper is still the most widespread medium through which recorded information is passed. Electronic and optical databases may be increasing their role, but the paperless information society is still many years ahead. Computer output is still responsible for consuming considerable volumes of paper, but the proliferation of journals, papers, booklets and leaflets is continuing to increase. Much is due to improvements in printing technology that the microprocessor has brought, the latest innovation being the quality and presentation levels achieved through desk-top publishing. The quantity and variety of information that is now available in print has added considerably to the information explosion.

In the past, items that were not available locally could usually be obtained from the British Lending Library at Boston Spa, and they would often arrive as photocopies of the originals. While the operation of the Library is like the production line of a factory, there were often delays in the arrival of journal articles that were being sought with some urgency. Now, facsimile transmission is being used, and this method of despatching the information will make the receipt of documents much more rapid than in the past; more paper perhaps, but the use of this means of communication will be a growing one until such time as all relevant materials are stored in databases that can be examined electronically. Copies of rare documents or protected originals can be made available in this way all round the world at minimum inconvenience. Despatch can take place at times when costs are low or across time-zones, as the machinery at the receiver's end can respond automatically.

Apart from facsimile transmission or computer print-outs, communication through paper is dependent on the traditional post and delivery systems. The receiver is identified and known to the person sending the material. With broadcasts, however, such pinpointing of people listening or viewing is not so precise, although various scrambling or coding of messages can ensure that only certain people can understand them. Radio is a much neglected communication system, but the technology is increasing its versatility. Signal receivers can now be built that will assist in tuning the radio and then respond to identification tones that switch on and record a programme that the user requires. At the end of the broadcast, the set will switch off again. Digital data can also be transmitted by radio.

Once received, the programme can be replayed from the cassette at any appropriate time. Miniaturisation and the microprocessor have been forces behind the development of the ubiquitous portable cassette player, the earphones which so many people now use to isolate themselves from their environment. These will replay the broadcasts just as any purchased or home-recorded tapes.

At present, television broadcasts cannot be switched on for recording in the same way, but the capability is likely in the future. However, there are an increasing number of channels, all transmitting information of potential value to the people receiving it. Coming from all over the world by satellite, the amount of video information available will continue to grow rapidly, and it will be accessible to all those within the footprints of the various satellites, provided they have the requisite dishes.

Apart from programmes in the general sense, satellites will also provide users with a means of video conferencing between countries, transferring data, pursuing some interaction through radio or telephone communication to the transmitting station. Some satellites have specialised functions such as weather watching, surveying and photographing the ground, undertaking measurements for various scientific experiments and so on. The signals from these, the so-called remote sensing satellites, are all receivable across the country; with the appropriate equipment and software the data can be translated into usable information.

Cable television is not widespread yet but, particularly in high population areas, its presence will grow. More channels will be available through cable, and all the facilities that can be provided through broadcasts will be accessible. In addition, interactivity with the transmitter will be possible, although the level will depend on the demand and the amount that the owners feel is economically justifiable. In theory, programmes can be started and transmitted at the time the user requires, and the user can also control the remote video player. In practice, however, such facilities are very unlikely to be on offer to a general audience, although selected study sites may have access. In theory also, a complete video link-up between members of the audience in their homes and the studio presenters can take place, but again in practice such a facility is unlikely to be made generally available.

Video recording is also possible from cable just as it is from national transmissions and satellite relays. Together with videodiscs and purchased recordings, these form a substantial extra dimension to the stored data that can be accessed by users. Recordings provide the facility for stopping and starting the viewing under the user's control, undertaking it after appropriate preparation and with any suitable accompanying material. Amateur recordings are now used frequently to provide visual evidence of events which the professional broadcasters missed, and so many current and future historical resources will be available only in this way. In business, at work, in scientific experiments and in the environment, video is becoming an increasingly important recording medium for analysis, debate and sharing information.

This survey of a selection of some of the current and future developments in communication, taken with the various mechanisms for accessing databases described in the first part of this chapter, demonstrates the growth in accessibility to information of all types and the increasing amount of it that is available. If the most obvious and widely discussed are video channels, they have to be noted as the means by which most people receive their information. Through satellites, and maybe through cable, the variety of international and local information sources that will be accessible will be extensive and form a rich potential source of aids to understanding and learning. Foreign broadcasts are popular in every country, and their use directly or indirectly encourages understanding of different national perspectives as well as language learning.

Dialogues with people in other countries are one of the values of electronic mail (email). Valuable as conversations over the telephone may be, they tie people to places and times which are not necessarily convenient. Electronic mail exchanges can take place at times which the user and receiver each choose separately. The use in education is growing, as both teachers and children find value from the system. There are database facilities as well, mentioned above, but the use of electronic mail seems to include the following activities:

1. *Exchanging messages between schools and groups of children.* Usually,

these relate to activities or gaining information about a contrasting environment.

2. *Sharing data.* Schools have been exchanging data about their history, local community, regional behaviour patterns, and in an international context national data. Some of this data is in a form which can be used in a local computer program or may be the program itself.

3. *Undertaking joint projects.* Children can be involved in developing aspects of projects in different schools. Assignments and projects are important parts of studying, and doing them with others in different schools can add a new dimension. Science work, experiments, field work, and different views of the same historical event are all aspects of study that are taking place between schools in individual countries and internationally.

4. *Stimulating the learning of languages.* Exchanges between schools in different countries is leading to an increase in the understanding and use of foreign languages. The dialogues are not just pen-pal letters – they are not textbook exercises either, but relevant and interesting discussions of behaviour and attitudes that motivate language learning.

5. *Writing newspapers.* Much interest has been aroused in the preparation of newspapers in school from material gathered from official news media and other schools, and circulated through electronic mail. The output is printed using desk-top publishing software. Whether for newspapers or magazines, the use of the electronic mail system to gather material nationally and internationally has valuable educational benefits.

6. *Developing curricular materials.* Teachers are using the system for sharing ideas and developing materials in collaboration with colleagues in different parts of the country. There are also international examples of this work. Teachers are also using the system to share ideas for project titles.

Electronic mail provides a range of opportunities for exchanges of material and questions between schools and other countries, and this expands the extent to which children and teachers can have access to information and share it. The technical procedures also introduce some key principles, including the issues of privacy, the value of sharing, the use of records, the range of essential data, the issue of authorisation, and the technology of linking systems.

An extension of electronic mail is computer conferencing. It is not the same as email, which is like a letter directed to an individual or a named group of people receiving the correspondence privately. Conferencing is targeted on a mass audience – all those who decide to join in the discussion. All the dialogue between the participants is open to every-body, although this does not prevent individuals from using an email facility to send private correspondence if they so choose. Each confer-ence relates to a particular topic, and one person (probably the initiator) takes on the responsibility of monitoring and guiding the discussion. Unlike face-to-face discussions the conference runs over extended time, and participants can spend hours or days considering and preparing their contributions.

This is an ideal system for distance learning, a different form of debate but one which can support the development of ideas and argument and lead to greater understanding. Conferencing is also useful in more conventional circumstances, for example where a section of a course is over but both teacher and students wish to continue thinking about certain issues. This is also helpful at school level, where the marshalling of ideas and arguments is an essential skill that has to be developed in later years. However, the distance learning option is the area in which it is likely to see most growth. There is no need for a conference to be linked to a course for it is just as beneficial, for example, in sharing research developments, exchanging views on methods of business presentations, or sharing thinking on political issues.

The new opportunities that the technology has brought to the access and collation of information and the opening up of communication are of considerable value to distance learners, and indeed to all those using open learning techniques for their study. Whether this is in the school environment, using supported self-study techniques, or working from home, the ability to tap into sources and communicate with peers has provided a much wider and more supportive atmosphere than has previously been available. For those who have less favourable home facilities, a library could be appropriately equipped and perhaps designated an information centre.

Such are the opportunities that these technologies now provide that the whole balance of life could change. A great number of people now rush into the centre of London to buy and sell stocks and shares, but given a suitable terminal there is no reason why a significant proportion of this activity could not be undertaken elsewhere. Most involves computer exchanges of information, bargains and deals; much of the rest is based on telephone conversations. Doing this from home is, technically, perfectly possible although the atmosphere may be different and perhaps more relaxed. If the broker feels it to be important that the neighbours see him going to work, then driving to a suitable layby and using radio telephones would almost certainly provide all the necessary facilities in the very near future!

Effects on different subjects

With new sources of information and different communication systems have come new opportunities for the learner to access and use materials to develop knowledge. Information and activities that could not be contemplated in a practical way before have now become possible. The richness and diversity of information from all parts of the world are more accessible and usable now than at any time before.

New forms of expression and presentation have also been introduced, for example with electronic mail and computer conferencing. Dialogues through these formats lie somewhere between the informality of conversation and the formality of carefully constructed prose.

Sentences are usually complete, unlike free-flowing conversation, but the use of a formal essay approach would appear stilted and uneasy in the context of a mail item or an argument. The purpose of these dialogues is not necessarily to cause the receiver to create a hardcopy print-out but to read quickly and easily the sense of an argument, idea or message, and then to either respond or be stimulated to develop personal ideas and perceptions over a period of time. Anything too formal or closely argued inhibits the free and easy discussion or debate that is taking place. Of course, email is also used to exchange papers and similar materials and these are expected to be stored and formalised, but the general use of the system as a mechanism for exchanging news, information and ideas requires a more superficial approach.

Thus, videotex systems like teletext and viewdata are compressed journalism in their presentation, demanding a conciseness and shorthand that expresses breadth and detail in a very few sentences or notes. Databases can have information displayed through graphics much more easily than before, and indeed prose, graphics and numerical charts will be mixed in presentations prepared with the technology. In the future children and students should also be submitting material in electronic form rather than as print-outs. Some of these may include visuals from videodiscs as part of the 'essay', perhaps linked with text but using software to select and arrange the pictures in particular ways.

None of these changes is difficult to accommodate within education. Indeed, the breadth and variety of approach they introduce add a richness and diversity to communication that has been absent until now. The technological changes are not reducing quality but introducing a range which extends the opportunities for understanding and communication. For those who have had difficulties in working within the fairly rigid parameters of traditional education, there is hope that the options now on offer will give them more chance to contribute and display their abilities. There is much anecdotal evidence to support this, but objective research is needed.

To learn, children need to process information and shape it into knowledge. Learning cannot be drummed into a child, unless it is memorisation of data that is required. Children do not necessarily find it easy to accept the particular approach to learning a topic adopted by a teacher, which may be inappropriate for them. Successful learning, however, takes place when children develop their own strategies and patterns for organising, relating and manipulating information into knowledge. That comes from practice with information, which the appearance of the technology has made very much easier in every subject and at all levels.

The technology encourages a research-based approach to topics. So much information is now accessible that in every subject children can develop a hypothesis, examine the information and evaluate it to find whether there is sufficient evidence from which to draw a conclusion. The new GCSE examinations support this method of learning through their considerable emphasis on projects and assignments – an extension of the primary school tradition of topic-based work, where as the children mature more is left to them to organise and undertake. Again, the emphasis is on developing methods and strategies that are recognised as such and transferred to other fields.

One interesting feature has been the growth of co-operation in dealing with this research-based approach. Children in primary schools worked together on topics, all contributing their respective parts, but assignments in secondary education used to be dealt with individually. Now, team approaches are frequently being encouraged, peer group analysis and insights being considered an important contribution to the growth of individual understanding. While this introduces many difficulties and problems for assessment, there is valuable enhancement to motivation and mutual support from this approach. Science, geography and home economics, as well as the humanities, all provide examples of this approach, not just in the strictly practical areas but also in development of the more theoretical dissertation. While the technologies have certainly not caused this trend, their appearance has assisted in sustaining it through the easy way in which joint exploration of information can take place. Collaboration with children in other schools, at home and abroad, is also encouraged through such techniques as electronic mail and conferencing to further enhance the approach.

The technology supports the exploration of data to create new associations and thus the potential for new insights. In the early days, many interesting questions arose from examination of data provided by the census returns – for example the localisation of families and jobs in particular parts of a town, and the fluctuation of numbers in certain streets over time. Other investigations followed to attempt to explain the results that appeared – for example the ravages of diseases in tightly packed communities rapidly became apparent. The rise and fall of particular skills and trades were readily linked to changing patterns of lifestyle, and children quickly gained an insight into how a society and its behaviour are painted through historical evidence.

Associations between data from all types of sources can lead to similar work. Are there correlations between the size of the pupil of the eye and the times when an animal is active? Are particular poets more inclined to one line length or metre than another? Is there any relationship betwen the natural occurrence of ores and the value of related redox equations? The questions are infinite, and all can be enlightened through careful association of data, often best expressed through some form of graphical display. By having the data in a form that can be related to other collections, the technology supports rapid analysis so that insights can be developed. Without the technology, the time spent in acquiring and relating information would be so great that the object behind the exercise would have been forgotten. True the techniques would be practised, but maybe only once, whereas with the computer they are seen to be used many times and the effort is spent on analysing the outcomes of the relationships, not the business of generating the data.

Of course, collecting data and putting it into the computer is a technique in itself which children gain from understanding. The technology supports experiments that require the collation of data, and children can again see the results quickly without their enthusiasm being drained through efforts of calculation and presentation. Because the data have to fit into a structure that can be manipulated, children have to spend time carefully planning the categories and headings they are going to use and thus the data they need to collect. Some collecting may be done directly by linking the computer through sensors to devices that do the appropriate measuring – for example movement of materials under stress over time, or changing climatic conditions. Other collecting is done by children and recorded by them in a database program. One of my favourite examples was undertaken to decide the optimum conditions for the strongest conker, and as one who loved to play conkers as a child I wish I had been able to discover the answer then! (Ross, 1984).

Working with databases with children involves helping them to categorise and recognise patterns and relationships. In all subjects in the curriculum these are essential elements in learning and developing knowledge, for they help to create mental structures that facilitate memory and understanding. Thus, by using the technology as a stimulus to the formation of databases, a great deal of effective learning can be achieved.

Now that there is more interest in open learning in schools, loosely realised under the title supported self-study, the information and communication facilities of the new technology have added value by providing appropriate facilities. The importance of open learning in post-school education is increasing, in particular with the diversity of specialist courses and training required at times that do not match the normal institutional arrangements. As yet, the use of information technology in adding new facilities and dimensions to this approach has not been developed as far as it could be, but there are signs of progress. In particular, there are preparatory developments in computer conferencing, and satellite connections will prove to be of importance. At school level, the opportunity to introduce a significant use of the technology in supporting self-study activities is considerable, and in some places is already recognised as an important tool.

Out of school, children increasingly expect to find their information and even communications via screens and the technology. From newscasts in shopping malls to interactive video as a means of deciding calorific values of foods in shops, the technology is becoming an everyday mechanism for providing the raw data that help to decide actions. While adults find it more difficult to accept, for children it is the normal means of finding the information they need. The use of databases in school is a continuation, admittedly leading to greater depth and complexity, of the general environment of living. In every subject, children need to make use of databases in a progressive way, using all types to organise and obtain data and information. Methods of teaching may have to be modified to ensure that there are relevant exercises that stimulate such activities, but work with databases is now a prerequisite for modern life.

As the technology develops, the appearance of cheap but extensive relational database systems, already available in some activities, will become widespread. Then the techniques of association and manipulation that have been referred to earlier will lead to more interesting ideas and suggestions for further questioning. Linked to the development of expert systems, the ability of children to explore and analyse relationships between data will increase and has the potential of producing a very stimulating learning environment. At this stage, planning the most interesting and relevant content of these programs is the priority.

Role of the teachers

In such an information-rich environment, together with all the opportunities for wider communications, it is necessary to consider carefully the position of teachers. Theirs was the role of information provider, but this is much less important now as other sources predominate. Of course this role has not disappeared, for there will continue to be many occasions when the teacher will need to supply the data in setting the context, guide the learning and correct the misapprehensions. Rather, it is the depth of memorised information of a particular subject that a teacher no longer needs.

Fundamental to all teaching is helping children to recognise the strategies and methods they are using as they learn a particular topic. One aim behind this is to assist them in transferring these approaches to other subjects of study; in dealing with these new materials, this is even more important. The techniques of handling and using information are pervasive through all areas of study, although biases and attitudes necessary in the more scientific subjects are different from those needed in the humanities. However, as a fundamental set of skills and learning strategies, being able to deal with information is increasingly essential in order to cope with the growing volume of data. Helping children to understand the way in which they are doing this is therefore an important role for teachers.

In order to develop this awareness, teachers need to encourage the use of information sources, of which those using the new technologies are currently the most significant. Selecting the relevant items and assessing their value come high on the agenda of skills that need to be acquired, and therefore some time needs to be devoted to them.

Using databases to develop skills in categorisation and logical analysis has been seen in many classrooms. There are many occasions when the opportunity to do this occurs in most subjects, but it does need to be encouraged. For the teacher, the difficulty is to identify the level of intervention needed, and some understanding of the way in which a particular program works is helpful so that children's errors can be corrected by transferring files rather than laboriously re-entering data. Much has been written about the value of developing understanding through making mistakes and correcting them, and this is also true for appreciating the problems surrounding the categorisation of information.

One interesting development from databases has been the appearance of new ideas as a result of manipulating them. If children are allowed free rein to explore data and look for collations, then it is likely that strange results will emerge which have not been encountered by the teacher before. The response to this may be to ensure that nothing unexpected can possibly emerge by constraining the children's access to the data. Alternatively, the teacher can welcome this as an opportunity for children to develop strategies for analysing the implications of the results that have appeared. By involving themselves in the work, teachers can be partners in the study that follows, and demonstrate through the example of their thinking methods how such an issue can be approached.

Using information also has grades of complexity, and just as the general curriculum of any subject is expected to show progression, so also should any work with information in any particular subject area. One of the important keys to this progression, although of course there are others, is the level of validity and authority that is given to any piece of information. The point to be emphasised here is that work with information, whatever the medium or format in which it is stored, requires as much consideration within the curriculum as the progression of mathematical problems within that subject area. For the teacher, it is necessary to be aware of these levels of complexity, and to ensure that children are moving forward, taking account of their individual ability.

Information is a strange commodity. Certainly in its electronic form – but also in some other formats – you can give it away or even sell it, and yet you still have it yourself. You can still use and manipulate it and above all develop new ideas and interests from it. However, exchanging and sharing information is a valuable activity, more especially as it generates other views and ideas as well as encouraging others to offer theirs to you. By working with other schools in the vicinity, or elsewhere in the country or even internationally, wider perspectives are introduced to children. A child's environment is often closely defined by the school, and yet opened out second-hand through television. Sharing information is one way of appreciating the existence of other children with similar learning problems and needs in other localities, and collaborating with them adds new perspectives from other environments. Setting up such arrangements does create a great deal of work for the teacher but it adds a valuable dimension to children's work.

Collaboration on this scale is founded on similar co-operative learning within the classroom. Information should not be seen as a private affair, but rather as something that gains from being shared and discussed. Setting up a database is obviously a shared activity but issuing information from one could be treated individually. Just as the teacher has an important role in fostering out-of-school contacts for information sharing, so within the classroom there is the necessary task of encouraging debate and collaborative use.

Of course, information is available not only within the boundaries of the school. For many years teachers have been asking children to collect data from their locality and home environment, to seek information from the public library, and to talk to local specialists such as police, gas workers, or gamekeepers. The growing accessibility of electronic information stores, either from home computers or through libraries and information centres, adds to the repertoire of sources and activities that children can pursue. There is, naturally, the need to ensure that at least a high proportion of children have access to such facilities, either directly or through collaboration with a friend, but teachers should seek to build on this availability to ensure that children recognise that information is accessible everywhere and not just confined to the school or official learning environment.

Encouraging children to use information and recognise the strategies they employ are the prime activities for teachers, but there are also important roles in managing and guiding children to sources, as well as working in partnership with them in the exploration of new associations and ideas that develop from this work. While much of this is usual for teachers, particularly at a time when research-based learning is becoming a major feature of examination requirements, the concentration on handling and using electronic information and communication systems is new to many, has added new dimensions and has raised the level of importance of this work as fundamental to the skills which children need.

Conclusion

The present age has been characterised by the term 'information and communication explosion', and there is clearly a considerable growth in both fields. This is not confined to Britain, or to the developed nations, but is international in its impact. Nor is there any sign that a stable state has been reached. Indeed, the opposite is true: the growth of information is accelerating.

Education has to respond to this, not by requiring children to accumulate more information by pushing more content into the curriculum but by ensuring that they have the techniques to access, handle and use it as necessary. Knowing where information is may be helpful, but knowing how to select, process and use it is far more essential.

The balance between having the information stored locally in the school or in remote databases will change as the curriculum and funding of schools alter, but children need to experience both and be aware of the criteria that have been used in deciding which is the more appropriate. The information will be both verbal and visual. The latter has not been considered as important up to now as it has been so difficult to handle, but technological advances have altered that and the rise of digitised video will change the picture further. Methods for dealing with this will be essential, and again the balance between local and remote storage will need to be determined.

Finally, the accessibility of information from the non-school environment grows also, and the use of this has to be built into learning activities. Uneven distribution of the availability of tools to access this information has to be recognised and surmounted if some children are not to be disadvantaged, for as they grow older and the economic balance alters this unevenness will gradually disappear. The impact of this accessibility on the style and content of education in school has to be assessed and absorbed into the curriculum if children are to recognise the relevance of the activities that teachers require of them.

References

Hopkins, D (Ed) (1987) *Knowledge, Information Skills and the Curriculum* LIRR 46. The British Library, London

Irving, A and Gawith G (1984) *Informatters* Kit published by Loughborough Audio Visual Services, University of Loughborough

Marland, M (Ed) (1981) *Information Skills in the Secondary Curriculum* Schools Council Curriculum Bulletin. Methuen Educational, London

Ross, A (1984) *Making Connections* CET, London

Watson, J D (1968) *The Double Helix* Weidenfeld and Nicolson, London

Chapter 3

Using the Technology

Introduction

The last two chapters have been concerned with using the technology in the classroom, but in this chapter I want to consider some of the implications of its use as an aid to teaching rather than just as the technology itself or as a means of collating and communicating information. In the last chapter, I stated that the technology really had only three effects: a mechanism for controlling the environment, for organising and storing information, and for communication. This chapter is concerned with (a) another aspect of information - dealing with it where it has been pre-processed by a producer, and (b) another aspect of communication - new methods of presentation.

Learning is concerned with the processing of information, in whatever form it is presented, and in this chapter it is information processing through computer-related materials with which I am concerned. This is only one form of presenting information - a very powerful method but just one of several means. Books and the talk of a teacher are two others among the many forms available. It is important that the new technologies are seen as further resources in the bank for a learner to explore and use, rather than as a total replacement. That the technologies have a great deal to offer the learner that is not so readily available by other means does not infer that the others must be replaced, although it is likely that many will become less widely used.

Communication is the other side of learning. If wisdom is just developed internally and not communicated, no-one else benefits and nobody knows about it. One of the tragedies of physical handicap is that sufferers often have considerable knowledge and wisdom but their disabilities prevent their communicating with other people. Through these new technologies some of these imprisoned minds have been given the opportunity of expressing themselves, and amazing have been some of the results. Details of this work are outside the scope of this book, but within it is the value of using mechanisms of this technology in providing children with new ways of communicating and presenting their ideas and understanding. Again, it is necessary to emphasise that these methods do not replace traditional mechanisms. Wordprocessors do not remove the need to use a pen, although they do reduce the necessity to use it as often. These are additional mechanisms – very powerful, but extra members of the battery of communication systems that an individual can use.

The range of approaches

Software is often divided into two main kinds: *generic* (or content-free) programs, and *subject-specific* ones which are those whose content directs them purposively towards supporting learning of a particular subject. For convenience, it is probably easier to deal with them separately, and that is the approach I have adopted below. However, there has been a tendency in recent years to suggest that generic programs are of greater value to teachers than the others, the argument being that teachers have a facility with which they can do what they like in order to help children, undictated by the ideas of a producer, particularly a commercial one. Whether this view is held for educational reasons, I am not sure. However, it is also true that the costs of generic software are much lower than subject-specific programs as the potential audience is much larger, and therefore they are a more economic proposition.

The argument does seem to be misplaced, however, for the good subject-specific program can prove to be very useful educationally. Inflicting on teachers merely a mass of content-free programs also encumbers them with a great deal of extra work in preparing software for particular areas. It also suggests that there is nothing to offer in science or geography but open shells. We do not expect the teacher to work from content-free textbooks, which are of course bound sheaves of blank pages, nor is there any suggestion that teachers should not purchase and use prepared worksheets. Confronted solely with content-free worksheets (that is, plain pieces of paper) a great deal of time and effort would be required to prepare a course, resources which few, if any, teachers have available.

The answer is not one or the other, but a judicious mixture of generic and subject-specific materials. Neither is better than the other. For any particular class confronted by a particular topic, a particular teacher will select certain resources as the most appropriate, and sometimes these will be generic, sometimes subject-specific. For that teacher, what is important is that both, not just one type alone, are in the bank of resources.

Generic software.

Programs that turn the computer into a control system and databases are two examples of this content-free software; they have been discussed earlier so are not included here. The main examples to be discussed are spreadsheets, wordprocessors, Logo, music creation programs, graphics, painting, design and other presentation systems. While some have natural homes in particular subjects, they are all useful in many, if not all, parts of the curriculum. The purpose behind the name 'generic' is that the software should be open to many different uses in many subjects, according to the needs of children and not confined to any special area.

Spreadsheets were one of the early types of program developed for microcomputers to prove their value to business, the Apple Visicalc being a very successful original piece of software. In education, however, they have been generally neglected although they are one of the easiest programs to use to explore the 'what-if' issues. Used in maths and science, for example, values for functions, properties of materials, speeds of reactions, and molecular and physical dimensions can be altered and the effect spread through resulting developments to see what happens. In home economics, changes can be made in menus and the impact on a week's food intake noted, or personal budgeting can be similarly examined. Geographers can use spreadsheets to consider the varying impact of rain and snow falls on the height of rivers, while in religious studies changes in population densities can be used to examine the impact on numbers and distribution of churches. Economic awareness is now such a feature of all activities that spreadsheets provide an excellent mechanism for examining the related balances between acquisition, expenditure and budgets in almost every subject, and not just the obvious ones of economics and business studies.

Preparing a spreadsheet demands logical planning and an appreciation of the formulae that describe relationships between different features. Having conceived these relationships, children are able to see the result of their hypotheses almost immediately because the computer does the calculation at high speed. The weight of the learning is on the parameters and their results, not the tedium of the calculation. Arranging the layout of a spreadsheet is not difficult, and encourages children to think of clarity of presentation and display. This can be further enhanced if the program is linked to a good plotter so that a graph can be selected and included.

Wordprocessors are now a widely accepted tool, some computers being purchased solely to gain access to such a facility. Different levels of program are available for different ages and abilities of children, and they have proved especially useful in helping the handicapped to communicate. Together with desk-top publishing facilities, the wordprocessor has provided the potential for turning every child's piece of writing into a polished and presentable publication. Now that spelling checkers and thesauri of synonyms and antonyms are available, the words can be correct and selected from a variety. Using these in school, however, has to be carefully planned in order to choose when the written results are more important than the verbal knowledge and creativity.

This generic program finds uses in every subject, whether the work is being done in English or a foreign language. Because children can receive a hard copy of polished work, there is a concomitant pride and satisfaction from the effort that has been given. If a WYSIWYG program (What You See Is What You Get) has been used, there is improvement in presentation as well, for amending it can be done with a few keystrokes. Writing can be collaborative, usually with considerable improvement in the results. Many gains in language ability, sentence construction, paragraphing, variety of phrasing and persistence in creativity have been described by teachers using these programs with their classes. Mostly this results from the ease with which the laborious writing and correcting can be achieved; turning a sentence around does not mean rewriting the whole piece again.

NATE (National Association for the Teaching of English), while agreeing that 'there is little doubt that word processors do have great value in the English classroom', suggests that the revision and correction features of the program should be used with care as they can remove freshness and spontaneity from a piece of writing and raise barriers in children. They also remark that:

> ...when three or four children are sitting around a computer, they have a natural focus for their talk, which encourages them to listen, reflect and participate. Some experience suggests that, used in this way, the computer can reduce the teacher's management problems and allow children to take a greater responsibility for their own work. The teacher becomes a helper, even a co-learner, rather than an assessor, because the computer itself is non-judgemental. Where the words on the screen are agreed by a group, the technology can encourage exploration and risk taking. (NATE 1986)

Logo is a computer language, and perhaps it is strange to include it under 'generic software'. However, it is constructed for easy understanding and use, producing results on screen and, if required, with a floor turtle or other devices from simple programming that can be mastered by children of five years and upwards. Variations have been produced that can be used in control technology and with music with similar simplicity. Short pieces of program can be tried on screen, corrected and improved until the desired results are achieved, and then the tools attached can be activated.

Working with Logo has proved exciting and stimulating for many children, and descriptions of this are widely recorded by the British Logo Users Group and in other publications. However, like so much advocacy for new programs, Logo suffered an excessive amount of 'hype' when it first appeared in Britain. It is a very useful system for gaining the first principles of programming, for appreciating the value of learning through iteration, for stimulating logic, thinking, reflection and collaboration, and even for considering design. The connection between 'design and make' is also rapidly appreciated at a surprisingly young age. However, it can prove very time-consuming for relatively little progress if a coherent and structured plan of work is not conceived, and if teacher intervention is not judiciously introduced. Older children can use the language to explore the relationship between functions and graphical display very simply. Other languages could be chosen, many advocating similar short Basic programs, but it has been well argued that mathematical expressions are much more clearly understood with Logo.

Music and painting programs provide children with facilities to express themselves in another medium. They are not replacements for playing a violin or painting in water colours, but another medium in which to express feelings and communicate ideas. As much popular music is now created electronically, the use of computer programs, possibly but not necessarily linked to other equipment, provides facilities which appear relevant and also overcomes the lack of performance skills in handling musical instruments which many children have. The computer can also be used to monitor the playing of these instruments and help children to improve their techniques. Composition too can be facilitated, the notes being tested as they are written.

The range of colours available with painting programs is increasing, and they can be altered and toned as necessary. As with any medium, the physical facilities introduce their own limitations, a pixel being the smallest 'dot' that can be differentially coloured, but there are also additional features such as animation that can be introduced to extend the scope of the imagery. Correction and alteration is relatively simple, down to the ability to change each individual pixel, and as with music programs the system provides the 'ham-fisted' child with a means of creative self-expression which previously may have been inhibited by poor motor skills.

Graphics and drawing programs have introduced similar facilities. Function graph plotters are one form of this software, helping children to explore the meaning of mathematical expressions or providing a mechanism for understanding the results of their own science experiments. Using ordinary graphics programs, children can easily experiment with display and presentation, changing and amending to create a result that communicates better or forms the outline for a creative piece of work in another medium. Such designs may even be in three dimensions, and rotated for examination. With computer-aided design programs, this can lead to output on plotters that may be directly reproduced, for example as printed circuit boards. Linked instead to lathes or other construction tools the output may be turned, for example, into pieces of equipment, sculptures, moulded plastic or textile designs, all a form of computer-aided manufacture.

All these creative programs remove some, if not all, of the physical problems of producing without inhibiting the planning and imaginative elements. The physical attributes may distort them, but good results can be achieved. Indeed, as the software improves it gets closer to offering unlimited possibilities. The work on the screen and within the program is what emerges on any print-outs or structure that is created, and repeatedly so, although it may be planned that it should remain for screen display alone.

Teletext programs are designed for use with screens alone, based on the broadcast information page design. Limited in capacity per page, the exercise of creating a succinct and yet attractive message is a lesson in itself. The mixture of graphics and text is used to convey messages within a school as well as being a method of publishing children's own work. Creative design is at the core of the good use of this type of program, and it provides a useful mechanism for encouraging self-esteem and confidence. Most subjects gain from the use of this and the graphics programs, giving children alternative means of communicating their ideas or conclusions.

No attempt has been made here to cover all generic software, but the chief ways in which they are currently conceived have been mentioned. Some people would also include programs that control, for example, interactive video presentations, but this can be considered analogous to a mixture of a database, a control program and a wordprocessor. Indeed, most other examples of generic software can be categorised as a mixture of some of the others.

Role of the teacher

For the teacher, there are several roles of play. Naturally there is that of providing technical guidance on using the programs and solving any problems that may arise. As with most educational programs, this does not mean being a computer scientist but merely being acquainted with the facilities and how they are controlled. Children usually have difficulties with a manual and need human interpretation!

There are also the usual roles that a teacher assumes when helping children to use materials. Activities such as stimulating them with ideas, commenting on and praising the work being done, suggesting alternatives or better methods of handling details are common to all creative learning, and the fact that a computer is involved does not alter this in any way. Similarly, as children progress, questions have to be raised to help them to develop their thinking and understanding, and at times the teacher will intervene more actively to guide the work into new directions or even produce some short cuts to speed up progress. Again, this is done with most practical work and is essential if the creative approaches stimulated by these programs are to be used to advantage.

More particularly associated with these programs is the need to help children to select the one that is most appropriate to their abilities, noting their personal progress and increasing the complexity at a suitable pace. Reminding them of the various choices they have within the facilities of a program helps them to vocalise and explain the reasoning behind those selected, and that is important in deepening understanding of the rationale behind creative decisions. Layout and colours are obvious areas in which this can take place, and the ease with which words or phrases can be changed throughout a piece of text leads to discussions of these in a similar way.

Finally, there is the important role of drawing out skills and learning techniques that have been achieved. No progress is made unless children recognise and understand their methods, although they will often be unable to describe them. However, internal recognition is important, and it helps transfer to other topics and subjects.

Subject-specific software
Programs in this group are designed to be used with a particular topic. Many of the most interesting and stimulating are open-ended and lead to similar aspects of creativity that are fostered by the generic programs described above, but the concept in the mind of the producer is linked to a subject or topic.

The drill and practice program is where most educational software started. These programs were relatively easy to write; they fitted a didactic curriculum and were readily assimilated by teachers into their current practice. In America, they were referred to as computer-assisted instruction (CAI), and dominated the use of the technology for many years as they were helpful in mastery learning and testing.

Essentially, the programs provided a small piece of instruction coupled with a series of tests, the answers to which had to be entered correctly if the computer was to recognise them. In many examples, such as table testers, the instruction part was missing as it was assumed this had been learned in other ways. The most advanced forms were designed along the lines of programmed learning, teaching a bit and then testing before moving on to the next. If the design was clever, remedial loops were introduced so that failures could be corrected.

Apart from the much cited reasons that they did not take advantage of the power of the computer and allowed it to control the child, such programs did not feature highly in education in Britain for very long. Children soon tired of them, however jazzy and exciting the graphics that accompanied the testing, but more significantly teachers felt that most of this kind of work could be done as successfully, if not better, by other means. As it was an effort and often expensive to employ a computer, the other methods were less arduous and were therefore the ones chosen. For those teachers who were concerned to move learning methods into the research-based approach, such programs were of no assistance anyway.

Yet they must not be totally dismissed. They have some value in revision, and children get value from designing their own tests and quizzes within an open framework of such a program in order to try them out on their peers. Drill and practice programs have also proved of considerable value in remedial classes and for slow learners where the patient computer is able to work in privacy and provide a form of reward for success. This builds confidence and also knowledge in children who frequently give up in its absence.

However, with regard to the scope that this technology offers in providing new learning opportunities, drill and practice programs have little to offer. It is unfortunate that this lesson is still not appreciated by many people facing new facilities from the technology. Early interactive video productions were designed on the lines of programmed learning and were very boring as a result; some material linked to CD Roms suggested questions and answers as a means of using it.

Tutorial programs never sought to test success. They were designed to provide an interesting way of examining a topic, even exploring it in a limited way and giving occasional problems on which the learner could prove understanding. However, their principal purpose was to assist in understanding a particular activity. The presentation was locked to the layout and approach adopted by the producer, and the program was a resource like an alternative textbook for the teacher to employ if a particular child found some difficulty with the standard presentation.

These programs have been quite successful when used for their real purpose, and teachers have not expected or sought more from them. Most use animated graphics, usually on several screens which can frequently be interchanged in different orders. Behind the presentation is a model, but the child's ability to amend the parameters is usually very limited. Some examples include the mechanism of transpiration in leaves with changing humidity, the erosion of cliffs with changing winds and rocks, the scaling of maps with changing types of presentation, the pathways of light into the eye with changing lenses, the design of kitchens with changing positions of furniture, or the menstrual cycle with changing levels of hormone.

Ideally, such programs are used individually or in small groups where they merit some discussion of the effects being seen. The approach can reinforce knowledge gained from other sources, offer a new angle to develop some understanding or provide a different form of presentation that helps revision. The BBC has introduced audio synchronised programs, those developed for secondary level work being essentially tutorial. The computer program is animated to link with the audio commentary, and as long as the timing is kept the same there is no reason why teachers should not record this if the sound of their voices are considered helpful for the learner. In practice, these programs have proved useful in giving a different means of access to a topic for children who have found the original explanations difficult to grasp.

Like all good programmed learning, these programs have often been field tested exhaustively before release. There is little evidence that much change results from this, and sometimes such trialling removes spontaneity and life from the presentation in order to prove more acceptable. Costs are raised and availability delayed. Similar field testing rarely occurs to the same degree with textbooks, and there is probably little need to go to the extremes that some suggest for tutorial software.

Simulation programs are those that link most closely with the current research-based learning techniques of education. Open models and adventures are usually only variations of the same approach. The principle of this type of program is its openness to change and variation at the hands of the learner, a sort of expanded 'what-if' approach in which the parameters can be altered to a considerable extent, and even the central algorithm amended if it is considered inadequate to the model. The activity of the program is dependent on the input from the learner, and there may be several as the simulation progresses.

The purpose behind this is to encourage exploration of the effect of changing the conditions within which the simulation works, and to uncover any relationships, patterns or interconnections that help to develop insight and understanding of causes and consequences. Change the size of any army and what is its effect on a war? Alter the altitude of an aircraft and what is its effect on fuel consumption? The success of a simulation is dependent on the degree of curiosity that the child has in the issue being explored. Developing thinking is dependent on questions that the child raises, and the manner of the exploration. The process is the acquisition of evidence to support or refute a hypothesis. Often there is no correct answer - merely a trend or a weighted tendency.

If the simulation is not apparently relevant, it is very unlikely that there will be sufficient curiosity to encourage learning. However, there is an inexhaustible range of possible ideas in every subject that should enable most topics to be considered in this way. For example, programs simulate power stations and the national grid, chemical extraction plants, running a farm for a year, feeding cycles in crops, pollution in a river, deciding on a place for a settlement, political decision making prior to various conflicts, managing a business, running the national economy, preparing a theatrical production, running a disco, visiting a foreign town, or floating in space. All are open to changing parameters which produce different effects, but through the experience of observing the consequences some insights emerge. Sometimes they are related to understanding the relationship between a particular cause and effect;

sometimes skills like decision making and problem solving are developed and practised; sometimes it is the social or human balances that are seen as crucial. The list of skills, strategies and understanding that can emerge from using simulations is long.

The trouble with simulation programs is that they seem large and complex. Less able children may find that too many varying parameters are confusing and inhibiting rather than helpful, and it may be necessary to start with only a few and switch in others as understanding and confidence develops. For some children, going beyond a few may not be comprehensible and the simulation should be stopped there, whereas other children will examine the issue in greater and greater detail.

Nor is there any need for a simulation to be very large. Creating different graphical effects in mathematics by changing the value of functions can be done in a very short program and lead to a considerable amount of understanding. One of my favourite problem-solving programs was based on determining the relationship between the number of sides of a polygon and the number of diagonals that could be produced. The learner entered the number of sides together with an estimate of the diagonals. On the screen, the real result appeared. After several attempts it was possible to examine the results and deduce the relationship. A graph could also have been drawn to do this. Knowing the relationship was not important and I have already forgotten it, but developing strategies to solve the problem was.

An addition to the generic programs is an empty simulation, adventure or model. The idea is that children and teachers can create their own, and this process will greatly enhance understanding for there is no better way of learning a topic than trying to teach it. Personally creating a simulation of photosynthesis is a very good method of exploring the interrelationships between physical conditions and chemical reaction. Producing one's own dragons and demons adventure with logical problems is an excellent method of understanding the process of thinking. Using the resulting programs on one's peer group is a simple means of developing self-confidence and respect.

Expert systems at school level are only just beginning to appear, as more powerful computers with larger memories become available. The potential has been highly rated by advocates, but the examples are not there to prove it yet. Devising rules for a system is a useful exercise in itself as it requires a considerable amount of analytical thinking about an issue and careful examination of iterations from draft examples. There is also potential in assessing children's work and helping to direct them to further levels of difficulty as appropriate. However, this sophistication of the technique of computer-managed learning has to be examined in practice before the impact on the organisation of learning can be analysed. There is likely to be considerable value in helping learners to interpret the meaning of problems and identify the issues that need to be examined, and this would be an asset in research-based learning. However, the complexity of human responses and the processes and strategies of learning that need to dominate the curriculum in the future do not offer easy accessibility to analysis by an expert system. That suggests human assessment of progress will not be totally replaced.

Support materials are needed to accompany all these programs. For drill and practice they are likely to be relatively trivial, but the other categories of program are likely to benefit from more detailed offerings of support. These may be extensive textual explanations of contexts, background, derivation of models and further references.

Worksheets may be included for further activity with tutorial programs or for creative work with simulations, particularly at primary level. Teachers may find that producing their own fits the programs more closely into the context of the programme of work the children are tackling than anything published.

A computer program must not be considered as a self-standing exercise all on its own, but planned as part of a continuous period of work. It provides a resource or, in the case of the generics, a tool which helps children to develop their knowledge but within a context. Learning out of context is usually dismissed as frivolous or irrelevant, but taken with other resources and in other settings it forms part of a total environment in which a particular topic is explored and developed. Support materials, whatever their form, are important in helping to establish this.

Role of the teacher
It is the teacher who plays the most significant part in ensuring that the context and relevance of the work is appreciated. As well as acting as technical support and problem solver, the teacher's role involves guiding the selection and use of programs in such a way that the children understand that the materials further their understanding of the topic being examined. By pointing out links to other materials, switching in further levels of difficulty, probing their analyses through questions, and stimulating their curiosity, the depth of study is increased. The assumptions behind a model within a simulation need to be examined and questioned too if they are not to be accepted at face value as expressions of the 'truth' merely because they are on a computer. The program was made by a human with all the prejudices and errors thus implied.

The most difficult roles are those of timing intervention and drawing out learning results. If the former is done too early, the process may not have gone far enough for it to be fully established. Waiting too long can lead to boredom within the limitations of the exercise. Yet some intervention is usually needed in order to help children, particularly younger ones, to learn to pace their work. Such interventions can be useful in drawing out the learning strategies that have been used, the thinking that has taken place and the personal skills that have been developed.

Selecting material

From a growing range of software, videodiscs and related materials, the teacher has to choose what to purchase or acquire. Making this selection requires two different kinds of criteria to be considered: objective and subjective. The latter involves three main areas: the content, the approach and the support. This section of the chapter considers these points.

First, the objective criteria associated with technical issues is considered. In essence, these can be summarised as 'Does the material work with all its facilities with the equipment I have available?' The guideline for users is not to take anything for granted. At the present time equipment is going through a fairly substantial transition which will not be complete for several years, and during this period materials will be made available in a wide variety of forms to meet the various types of machine and specification that are around in education. All the old machines have to be supplied, as they are still frequently in use, as well as all the new ones. To overcome several problems machines also use 'emulators' which are designed to make them behave like different equipment, and software is often marketed as being able to run under someone's emulator. Beware, for often it fails to do so, or some parts of its facilities do not work.

The best known of these emulators are those for 'BBC Basic' and 'IBM PC', and most have been cleverly designed. However, there are many BBC programs that do not run under these conditions, just as there are many PC programs that fail. You can be certain that 'improved' emulators will appear, and that there will be emulators for other equipment as well.

Therefore, just reading the advertising is usually not enough. Checking with advisers and other users, reading reviews and describing one's own configuration of equipment to suppliers are all helpful guides, but in the end the proof of the pudding is in the eating, and that means trying it on one's own machine. Problems are normally associated with the operating system, graphics and sound capability, resident memory, other on-board programs in ROM, and links to other equipment. Where video is involved, the digital or analogue forms can cause difficulties. Finally, it is always worth making sure that the right form and size of delivery system is used. With so many different types of disc it is not surprising that the wrong one is often purchased! If all this sounds confusing for the user, it is worth remembering that it is just as bad for the supplier!

So much for the objective criteria. Let us assume that it is possible to purchase material that will work satisfactorily on your equipment. The question is now whether it is worth purchasing. Will its use add value to the learning that the children undertake? The answer to that is subjective for it has to be useful for particular children working under particular conditions, and it is those criteria that will be discussed next.

First, there are those concerned with the content of the material. Given the normal assumptions that you, as their teacher, would expect children of the age with which you are concerned to find acceptable, the material must be reasonably accurate. It should be interesting and motivating for them. These materials are getting increasingly complex and extensive, and it really is not possible to go through all the facets to prove that they are accurate. When dealing with a textbook, you would not expect to read the whole of it before purchase, and you should treat the software in the same way. If strategic 'dips' show that the content is satisfactory, then it must be assumed that the rest of it is as well. If it is to be used in a primary school it does not require the depth and sophistication that may be necessary at degree level, but you must ensure that the level of language is appropriate for the age range of the users.

Next, the versatility of the software should be considered. The case for this is often exaggerated – certainly with subject-specific materials it is unlikely that the programs will be used repeatedly in every year of the school. Indeed, many teachers would think that would not be good practice. However, consideration should be given to being able to use the same material with children of different abilities, perhaps by varying the levels of difficulty and complexity.

This leads to the next criterion – being able to amend the program. Does one have to be an experienced computer scientist to change some of the words on the screen, or are they accessible to the relative novice? Where it encourages relevance the content and references in software should be local, but a complex piece of programming may make it impossible to change, for example, the name of the river from the Tyne to the Thames so that children could link their perceptions to it more readily. Amendments may be more fundamental: adjusting the algorithm to suit the approach to be used, redrawing part of the graphics or introducing variations for different groups of children. The support materials should not be forgotten either, as (for example) worksheets may require rephrasing. Links to other materials may be introduced, either within the support materials or as an extra in the program. It may be desirable to make changes in the links within a videodisc or similar material, or to encourage the children to do so.

Another potential change is to add a locally developed 'front end' – the way the screens look and are managed – in order to make it similar to other programs that the children use. Part of the difficulties that children, and other users for that matter, have is associated with the way in which the program is handled, and having a known system of access as the key to its use can help to overcome them. This is also the reason behind the next criterion: ease of use. Just how much difficulty will the children find working with the software? How much of their time will be spent learning how to make use of it? Will that time be well spent or wasted?

There are many different ways in which a program can be entered and used, some based on the stable of a producer, some devised at the whim of a particular designer. Some are obvious to the intelligent and experienced but very difficult and confusing to the novice, and at present all users should be considered as novices. Programs designed by or for Apple Macintosh computers all look very much alike, and users find it easy to move between them for the conventions are the same, but no other computer company has adopted that approach. For the rest, so many different suppliers of software are involved that there is no chance of compatibility. The present enthusiasm for 'windows', a technique for managing the contents of the program, has produced some similarities, but there are wide variations still.

An argument for international standardisation of some of these conventions has been made by many educators, and while the advantages are obvious there are implicit dangers in inhibiting development. The windows environment is an enticing one, but it still raises complexity through the use of individual icons as the graphic signals for particular actions. Rarely do companies use the same icons as others, and new ones are freely invented to meet new needs. Is it really envisaged that there will be international agreement on all icons (for there will be several hundred of them)? If a new need arises, will the new icon have to be accepted internationally? The problems are clear for icons, and the same will be true for the other parts of a configuration. Development and improvement comes through experiment and freedom to explore, particularly with such a new technology and such innovative uses. Some software that is much easier to use than the common windows is already available, and there is much more to do in developing this aspect of ease of use, the interface with the user.

However, the difficulties will continue for a long time. For example, how does a child know the mechanism for moving to the next screen? Various programs use different mechanisms – the space bar, key 'c' for continue, return or enter, yes or no, OK or cancel, touching or indicating a corner, and so the options go on. What about access to various options in a wordprocessing program: how are these identified? Some programs use the control key and a letter selected for its relevance to the option, others a function key, or an icon, or a part of a window, an item on a 'pull-down' menu, or a code letter at the bottom of the screen. Sometimes a message appears telling the user what will happen or can now be done, but in other programs there is no such help. Indeed if 'help' is typed in, the user may receive several screenfuls of often incomprehensible computerspeak, a message like 'no command', or a genuinely helpful piece of information. Colours are also frequently used as instructors. Indeed, the good use of colour is another aspect of the judgement that a teacher should use in measuring ease of use.

If the above paragraphs seem to expect a great deal from software – versatility, amendability, ease of use – not too much notice should be taken of all of them in every instance. The user may have no need to amend a piece of software, so the capability to do so would be superfluous. In raising them as issues, they are identified as criteria which should be considered but in the context of the approach and types of use to which the materials will be put. It is easy to overstate the importance of subjective criteria, for they are only necessary if they are relevant to the learning in which the programs will be involved.

The next batch of criteria is related to just this issue, for like textbooks and other learning resources there are many different types of educational arrangement in which they could be used. Some, for example programmed learning texts, lend themselves to particular approaches or situations, while others such as reference texts support different objectives and learning activities. The same is naturally true of the products of this new technology, and in selecting material there have to be conscious decisions made about their use. Is the design and style of the material appropriate?

Some of the questions that may be used in such an analysis are: Is the material to be used for individual study, group work, or with a whole class? What is the environment in which this learning may occur – the classroom, a special computer room, the library, home? The question of the level of available support then arises, for the home or even the library may not have sufficient specialist expertise to help a child. Does this matter? The quality and level of sophistication of the software will have a bearing on the answer to this question.

Then there is the approach that is needed to use the program effectively. If it aims at exploratory approaches, is this understood and recognised by the children who will be working with it? Can they handle working in such an open-ended situation? Indeed, can the teacher manage and support such an approach? Some simulations can stimulate a great deal of exciting learning, but with children who expect a didactic approach or a teacher who cannot produce an atmosphere in which this can be expressed, they can fail miserably.

Another question that should be examined is the presence and quality of support materials. For some programs these may not be necessary, but they are helpful for the majority of subject-specific items. They provide channels into further work, and may help to set the program in an appropriate context. Does the approach adopted by such materials match the one it is hoped to generate?

Perhaps it is difficult to recognise this in the time available to check through the software. Reviews and case studies of the use of the material are valuable, particularly those that describe different ways in which children exploit it to greatest advantage. Some teachers have created very imaginative arrangements and settings for the use of software, and these are often described. Many subject associations can now offer help.

Finally, in these criteria on approach, it is useful to consider what advantages the children will gain from the material. Is it fundamental to the learning arrangements of that piece of the curriculum, and in the teacher's view planned to enhance and improve understanding? Much software introduces novel ways of addressing a subject or of developing skills that are better than previous ways of teaching them. In some cases, it allows the exploration of topics that are not possible except through the use of this new technology. Obvious examples of this are dangerous scientific experiments and work with large databases in history.

On the other hand, the software may be considered valuable in extending or enlarging the area of work being studied. Vectors and forces can be understood theoretically, although children usually find them very difficult. The addition of simulations of experiments with objects falling in a lift shaft or moving in space can be helpful in illuminating and enlarging the vision and therefore the understanding of children, but they could not be considered essential. Of course, for some children they may provide the key to understanding the whole subject, and that is the great advantage of having a variety of resources available to help learning. If one is really concerned to see as many children as possible learn a topic, this is the approach to adopt for undoubtedly more of them will do so. On the other hand, if costs are to be kept down and a failure rate is acceptable, such materials would not be acquired.

The same judgement could be made of software to be used merely to enrich the learning of the children. Field work is important, but exploring a videodisc of the study centre at Slapton Lea, for instance, if you use another one is not essential and may not even enlarge understanding. It does, however, enrich the work on ecology. Exploring a simulation of battles of the First World War, for example, can enrich the knowledge of cause and effect but is not essential if it is not the child's area of study. Enrichment develops depth through other examples and experiences, induces confidence through using similar patterns of thinking in different subjects, develops interest because the examples are motivating and stimulating, but is not essential if the target is merely to pass an exam or reach a particular standard.

Approach criteria are very important in the subjective sense, because getting them right means that the material will match the atmosphere and environment that teachers are going to generate. Conclusions cannot be drawn by others, for only the teachers know their classes and how they wish to settle them into a learning framework. However, there are difficulties in appreciating all that can be achieved by a complex piece of software. As microcomputers increase in power, so the range of facilities and sophistication can be developed further, and it may be that different approaches can be used if material is entered from a different angle. The problem is finding out, and if there are no adequate reviews or case studies, time has to be spent in examining the material to discover its value.

Working through a program is a form of training, in this instance self-directed, and the final batch of subjective criteria that need to be considered in selecting materials relates to the training support the teacher gets with them. The more complex they are, the more important such support is. Sometimes this is self-directed, either through personal exploration or through guidance matter within the package that is specifically designed to help to work through the material and identify its learning potential. The incorporation of exemplar runs with a simulation can be very helpful in identifying the approach suggested by the producer, although it should not be felt that this is necessarily the only way in which the program can be used. When using books with a class, the teacher does not insist that the various chapters or sections are read in the order that the writer expected, but instead moves around to match the helpful parts to the particular needs of the children. Software is just the same, although there are consequences of certain actions with computer programs that do not arise from the inactive book.

The problem faced by the teacher is that of time. It can take several hours to get to know a program, even for the most experienced teacher, and time has to be set aside to do this properly. The more sophisticated the program, the more time is needed. Ideally, there will be an in-service course to accompany the introduction of such software, providing guidance from an experienced user together with time to try out various features. In its absence, the teacher has to make do with guidance that the producer has provided.

One of the benefits of in-service training is the discussion that takes place between peers about the program and its possible uses. Even if there is no course, discussions can take place between teachers in different schools about the style of using a program and its benefits, but this needs to be encouraged and stimulated. Much more successful informally where personal status and credibility are not threatened, such sharing of views and perceptions can be extremely valuable. Local branches of subject associations may wish to be involved, as may trade unions that have strong interests in training. Developing understanding of software is not dependent on the official in-service system, for other means are possible. The aim is to support collaborative thinking – not a particular mechanism.

The effects on subjects

Many of the uses and therefore effects of this technology have been indicated in previous sections of this chapter. However, another significant influence is the attitude of the teacher, and this section will be developed from that point of view. The attitudes described are not exclusive, for teachers can have different approaches on different occasions, but the immediate effect on the subjects will largely be dependent on the way in which the teacher encourages the software to be used.

'Just another resource for my subject'.
So many of the materials, particularly databases, can be viewed in this way. Every subject gains from faster access to information, and the speed is as important as the size of the bank of material that is available and so quickly sorted. Sometimes the information is visual, as in video stores of various kinds, and this provides another viewpoint to the topic that is being studied. If the teacher provides some organisation to the information, for example in the order in which parts of a videodisc of plants or reproductions of old masters are selected, then the child works through the material along predetermined lines and can develop a memory or thinking pattern that is typical of the usual treatment of the subject matter.

Many of the subject-specific materials can be used with the same attitude. Most tutorial software is thought of as another resource that children can use to help them to understand a particular problem, for example using a compass or practising titrations. Just as a video of *Twelth Night* brings alive a play that is being studied, so the animation of cloud formation gives a visual insight into an apparently theoretical cycle. This use of the new technology is a valuable one, supporting traditional approaches to the curriculum and providing new material to help children to understand it.

'It is very motivating'.

What teacher does not want such material, particularly in some of the secondary subjects? In some schools the technology is used in a computer room, and children feel there is something special about moving to such a place to study. With other equipment the expense is such that only a few examples exist, and using the interactive video equipment or the desk-top publishing kit is therefore something of a treat. Motivation is high when there is scarcity value! Much of the material is also pictorial and animated – better than learning from static turgid books – and frequently there is a fun element too. In an adventure game the maths problems that have to be solved help to locate a princess or cross a patterned floor, one piece of which will blow the pupil up if the equation is not solved and identified. Much maths is learned and practised from such an exercise, but it is also very entertaining.

It is not just the excitement of the equipment, the fact of it being a computer, or even the entertainment value which is important. Motivation is also generated by outcomes from some of the work. A drawing done by a Turtle, a nicely printed story written on the wordprocessor, a painting that is printed in colour on paper, a poem that is surrounded by graphic illustrations, an application of control that works, or a technical design that has been plotted, are all examples of work that would have been hard to do without this technology, hard not in the skill or academic sense but because of the time and tedium involved. All are also immensely satisfying and can be copied, by another 'print-out', and taken home to parents. For those with physical disabilities or who are just lacking in the appropriate dexterity, these are pieces of self-expression that could not be done easily in another way. Some of the outcomes can be printed as the School Newspaper through the desktop publishing system or presented on the videotext system throughout the school for all to see – an activity which helps to generate self-confidence.

For slow learners, the programs can present smiling faces when a problem is solved correctly and helpful messages to give guidance when it appears too difficult, and they will wait forever for the next key to be struck. This mixture of patience, support and praise are essential for helping slow learners to develop confidence and courage and to produce work which shows progress. While this encouragement can be given by the teacher, the time problems are considerable; with the help of the computer much more can be achieved.

'The world of information technology is opened up to them'. It is important that children are prepared for a future society in which information technology is a pervasive feature. Working with control technology mimics manufacturing processes in industry, as well as various household systems of security. In the office the spreadsheet, wordprocessor and database are dominant features, and in training at all levels the use of computer-based study and interactive video is now widespread. As home-based work continues to expand, the use of fax transmissions and electronic mail grows; using these systems for learning activities at school will help to make them so commonplace that they will be part of the background furniture. As for information, the dominance of computer systems for providing this grows apace, and the use of screens for its display is becoming the norm.

By using this technology in school and teaching about its commercial and domestic applications, children will gain a familiarity that will be helpful in their future. There is a sense in which such work can be considered vocational. Having some knowledge of the general applications and configurations of the technology may assist in helping pupils to discriminate when they have to make decisions in the future, whether at the level of purchasing for an office or factory or acquiring equipment for their own homes. Learning not to fall for every wheeze of a salesman can be a lesson of value, and that can only be based on knowledge and experience. However, this comes not from a set of theory lessons but from using the equipment practically, either to develop special knowledge as in computer studies or to use it to learn other subjects. Sometimes, a teacher may need to point out such features as memory, structures of data storage, or the meaning of keys such as 'return', but usually children will pick this up through the conversation of peers and the actual use of the equipment. Experience outside computer studies is useful in emphasising the breadth of application of the technology and some of the facilities that would be expected from a piece of generic software.

'It introduces new opportunities and options for learning that resolve problems'.
There are many pieces of learning which teachers have felt would be beneficial but which have proved impossible for various technical and physical reasons and which the technology has now made available. Several have been referred to earlier – drawing for the 'ham-fisted', music for the 'all thumbs', writing at greater length for the messy and unintelligible. Science experiments that could not be done for reasons of danger can be simulated and performed, while others that need too long a time can be compressed by simulation or monitored and managed in real time over several days. Experiments on interactive video can be used to take measurements. In the realm of data manipulation, research-based learning gains a great deal from access to information and its interpretation. Historical, geographic, economic, social and scientific data can be collected and analysed through appropriate programs, not only to speed basic fact-finding but also to correlate the data and generate new ideas.

If this access and use of information is one of the most significant results of the technology, another has certainly been the impact of modelling and simulation. From the youngest age, learning has been stimulated and excited by exploring possibilities and finding answers to the incessant drive of curiosity. What happens when children push their hands through sand? It is different from doing the same thing through clay and water, and creating shapes with these substances is different too. Lessons are learned unconsciously but firmly about materials and physical manipulation, which last throughout life and can only be understood at that age by doing it – not by hearing it explained. Dry sand castles fall down, but wet ones stay up longer. It does not matter why then, but the concept of the value of water is in place.

With simulations and models on the computer, the same exploration goes on. The 'what-if' experiments are merely more sophisticated forms of playing with clay, sand and water, but very much less messy. With the computer's speedy calculations, the results of changing the parameters, trying new values and testing the system happen almost immediately. There is no consumption of material and no danger. The effect of the passage of millions of years can be seen in seconds. Concentrations of chemicals can be changed at a simulated manufacturing plant and no expense is incurred, but the results can be seen. The rate of inflation can be raised on a model of the economy, and the effect on wages and interest rates a year later can be seen instantly. The contents of a house can be changed and the effect on costs and power consumption noted. Placing buildings in particular positions can affect wind and water movements on the animation on the screen, but no structures have to be created. Body movements can be filmed, digitised, measured and altered to analyse the effects on health and sporting prowess. Life in a Roman camp can be disturbed by the arrival of a legion, and the effects noted. All are calculated and displayed at high speed, although the results may not appear as numbers. These simulations are possible now because the computer can do the calculations quickly and display the different situations. No labour is required from the child – merely the experiment and the analysis of the results.

Nor is this restricted to specific simulation programs. Spreadsheets in particular, but other generic programs as well, offer the same facilities for trying things out. Neither the original data nor the model of the simulation are changed, but the effects can be seen and explored. These are new options for learning that have not been possible before the technology arrived, and they provide the teacher with facilities that overcome many of the old restrictions.

'The approach to the subject can now be changed'.
This is the most radical of the attitudes, requiring a positive commitment from the teacher. It is based on the premise that the technology offers facilities that support greater child-centredness in teaching, and encourage the trend towards the development of more autonomy for learning. The words 'development of more' are chosen with care, for complete autonomy is probably impossible and the degree of autonomy will vary from age to age. Nevertheless, if the development of greater personal responsibility for one's learning is accepted as a worthy target, then the technology is certainly a help in achieving progress towards it.

The emphasis will be on the child's use of the equipment rather than on the teacher's. Through appropriate programs and, importantly, other materials the child will explore and develop knowledge, usually by means of a project or assignment activity. Attention will be given to fostering curiosity and the development of personal thinking and learning skills, while the teacher spends time extracting interesting issues and helping children to recognise their skills, attitudes and achievements. This is possible with children of all abilities, not just the bright ones.

For example, using the design facilities of a program, children can create the pattern for a cloth, and then progress to using the equipment to control a loom to make it. The question could arise as to how this can be used in the home. Computer simulation can be used to arrange the furniture, move the walls and plan a domestic environment in which the patterns can be painted to suggest a relationship to others. The curtains, walls, carpet and chairs can be visualised in colour and the contrasts examined. Are the colours accurate? Comparison with samples can be used. Can the chosen design be afforded? Budgeting work follows, perhaps using a spreadsheet. Each child, or group of children, will prepare different analyses, will be asking different questions and will follow the examination and exploration in personal ways and at different speeds. Some may be diverted because a question interests them – for example the strength of materials made from mixed natural and man-made fibres which may lead to information gathering or even small experiments. Because of the technology, there is quicker access to information, easier manipulation of ideas and an ability to create outcomes in a form that can be used.

What causes irritation and conflict between people? Using a videodisc of situations, children can examine what might have created a particular issue: for example a domestic dispute between a married couple over money for a videorecorder. Role play and information gathering can deepen the understanding of the possible background to the problem. Issues such as the obligations of marriage, the balance of domestic budgets or the value of having a videorecorder can be followed up, using programs where necessary. The background data from the videodisc can be matched to the children's perceptions of the problem, and then a choice can be made from a number of alternatives as to what might happen next. From the videodisc the children see the producer's idea, but does it match their own? Are the producer's preconceptions and assumptions dictating a view that is unreal to the children? Through the technology this theme can be stimulated, with actors introducing a sense of reality and various alternative follow-ups made available to develop the situation. Also, the technology supports the provision of data and information about the background that can affect children's own researches. Further developments are infinite: for example the impact of changing laws on particular issues, which would stimulate a large amount of further curiosity.

Using a spreadsheet or a specific program, it is easy to create a description of the economic balance within homes in various settings. Altering the cost of food can have an impact on this balance, but *why* is it changed? The balance sheet of a factory can be affected by changes in the cost of the raw materials, but *how* does that happen? The balance sheet of the country can be affected by changes in the import bill, but *why* should that be? What analogies are there between these three situations? The speed of the technology makes it possible to play with and cross-relate these situations, with the children being concerned only with the impact on the balance sheets and not with the problems of calculating them. Information is necessary to build up the appropriate descriptions of influences, and there are many opportunities for developing other models, different forms of display and graphics, extensive openings for acquiring other interesting sidelines of thinking. Through the technology, the model can be developed and tested, cross-references established and the effect of several factors examined, all with concentration on analysis and little time wasted on calculations.

None of these examples could have been developed satisfactorily within reasonable time without the technology. Instead, children would have been told or shown in the order that the teacher determined, and only a certain amount of time would have been available in which understanding and learning could have been achieved. Even with this exploratory learning, time has to be managed but some must be available to allow curiosity to be roused and answers established.

This learning approach benefits from discussions with peers and teachers. Such collaboration can even include children from other schools, even other countries, and from it new perspectives and ideas will emerge. Information is at the base of the work, and it is developed by the children interacting with that information, working on and changing it, turning it into forms that they recognise on their terms. This is creative learning, responding to children's ways of thinking and not imposed from outside. The teacher manages the programme of work, supports and encourages the children, and ensures that they establish confidence in their own abilities. Such an approach can be taken without the technology, but there are considerable advantages in using it to extend the repertoire of activities in which children can be involved.

Interdisciplinarity

The divisions between subjects have been weakening for many years, and use of the technology is accelerating the difficulties in maintaining them. If transfer of skills and expertise is to take place, it is necessary for the divisions to disappear even further for their presence creates inevitable difficulties and barriers. English and mathematics have been part of most other subjects from the beginning, and there have been campaigns for 'English and maths across the curriculum' to try to encourage specialist teachers in ensuring that standards in these subjects are kept high in their particular disciplines. Marking the history essay for its English content as well as its history continues to be important. Nearly all subjects use graphics and elements of design in the presentation of work but I have not come across a 'design across the curriculum', so these campaigns are selective, concentrating on the traditional mainstream subjects and not those conceived as extras. Maybe this is the reason why although some British designers are among the best in the world, the general appreciation and support for good design is so poor.

Boundaries between subjects are disintegrating for many reasons. It is an obvious truism that knowledge is not naturally compartmentalised and that studies by children will expose this. In running a home or managing a business, one does not stop and say 'this is the home economics bit' or 'I need my knowledge of geography to visit my accountant'. The repertoire of knowledge is applied in a seamless way, and as more learning activities take note of the real world so the divisions are weakened further.

Many simulation programs raise this issue, because although they are designed with one subject in mind, their use and the learning that can be achieved may cover a number of disciplines. The 'Fishing Game' is concerned with managing a trawler to maximise the catch and ensure the best prices for it over a period of time. It was considered useful in biology, as some knowledge of the movement and reproductive cycle of fish is essential. However, the currents and conditions vary with the weather – meteorology, which is part of geography. Owning a trawler is a business: many of the decisions about when to fish and how frequently to return to port are elements of business studies and economics. Successful use of the program requires some maths ability in deciding which types of fish to look for, and students of home economics may have an interest in following up the quality and nutritional value of the catch.

Another simulation deals with the management of a river. Note has to be taken of the pollution threats and the different surges of water that appear in different seasons; various actions can be taken, although this depends on the level of the budget. This simulation was prepared for geography, but other subjects gain a great deal from it. The physics of current and erosion raise interesting problems and ecologists gain from consideration of the evils of pollution and its control. Chemists recognise the value in discussing factory outflows and methods of purification while those involved in business studies learn a great deal from the decision making that is necessary within a fixed budget.

Using computer-aided design software, children have been assigned the problem of designing the layout of a housing estate. Essentially this is a technology problem, concerned with materials and structures and, of course, design. However, the end result has to be financially profitable (see business studies), fit into the environment without damaging it too much (see ecology), and the style of housing and facility has to match the expected population (see sociology). Road planning has to be taken into account (see geography), and the effect on the broad economy of the area in which the estate is to be built should be noted (see economics). No estate can be developed without planning permission (see law), and its existence can have an effect on wind, rain, drainage and sunlight (see physics, geography, economics, biology etc).

The closer the problem or project is to real life issues, the more subjects are involved and the clearer it is that the divisions between them are not tenable. In the primary school, such divisions are not easily recognised by the children anyway, and the project- or topic-based approach happily transcends any boundaries that others might erect. They would be false, and there is no point in confusing the children. The examples above are selected deliberately from the secondary sector, where these divisions still assume some importance but where this type of material makes their continuation more difficult to sustain.

Information technology is therefore encouraging this breakdown because it supports the development and use of materials which are naturally interdisciplinary. Information itself cannot easily be packeted into monodisciplinary stores, and the large databases are so quick to access that there is no need to categorise the material into sub-directories associated with a particular academic area. Because the material is often of interest to and financed by industrial and commercial groups, such categorisation would be met with some disapproval.

As the trend of learning styles and approaches becomes increasingly exploratory and research-based, so the divisions between subjects will appear more artificial and unrealistic. Forcing them may indeed create more problems than it solves. One of the themes of this book has been the need to cultivate curiosity, and the chasing of answers knows no boundaries. The technology has not caused this breakdown of divisions, but the materials that are used with it are encouraging their demise.

Conclusion

This chapter has sought to demonstrate that the various uses of the technology have introduced new options for learners and teachers. From generic software to interactive video, new ways of approaching topics and subjects have appeared which can open more paths to enable a learner to acquire knowledge. While some applications extend the facilities that are available, the main underlining feature is that of 'what-if'. This unlocks the door to the opportunity for exploration and discovery at all levels and for all abilities.

If one of the difficulties of the future is uncertainty and change, the opportunity to explore at school and develop confidence is a valuable step towards being able to cope with it. Travelling into the unknown, being excited and curious about what is found there and then being able to deal with it, are useful lessons to experience.

It has been suggested that the technology opens the way to the replacement of teachers by software and training systems. In this chapter, changes in the role of teachers have been identified but in no case has their replacement been envisaged. With its present power and application, computers provide an extra mechanism in the armoury of tools available to the learner. Books, slides, worksheets, videos, broadcasts and verbal presentations will continue to be useful, side by side with the new technology. Through its interactivity and storage system, this technology is very versatile and offers opportunities that have not existed before. However, it should be seen as a mechanism, not a takeover.

It is the teacher who will place it in an appropriate position in the armoury of resources. The attitude and approach to learning adopted by the teacher will determine how important the technology appears in the scheme of the curriculum. Given unlimited software its usefulness can be considerable, but the degree and level that reaches will be decided by the kind of curricular approach that the teacher wishes to arrange and the freedom of action that the children are allowed. As the chapter describes, the impact of the technology on the style of learning can be extensive, but practical reality will be as the teacher permits and supports.

References

NATE (1986) *English Teaching and the New Technology into the 1990s.* National Association for the Teaching of English, Sheffield

Chapter 4

Administrative Advantages

Introduction

In a book that is concerned with the curriculum, discussion of the value of the technology to administration may seem out of place. However, all teachers would acknowledge that the smooth running of the administrative aspects of their work would relieve them of a great deal of pressure, and the time and energy so released could be devoted to teaching. The demands of administration have grown – many would say unnecessarily – and anything that helps to reduce them and put them in their proper place would be an advantage.

Child-centred teaching does, however, mean greater concern for the individual child rather than for the class as a whole and this, together with justified criticism of public examinations, has led logically to an enthusiasm for profiling – an administrative chore perhaps, but this method of recording the progress and development of an individual child can provide a fairer assessment and final reference. The arrival of computer systems makes it possible to maintain these records without too much difficulty and time-wasting.

Another aspect that benefits is the organisation of resources available for children to use in their learning. As the importance of a good background of information and learning materials becomes more apparent in new approaches and methods, so an effective administrative structure for them is more essential. The more individual the design of the curriculum, the more important it is to maintain a good track of progress ('the audit trail', as the accountants would call it) so that teacher and child have a better grasp of needs and targets.

The discussion in this chapter is therefore concerned with those ways in which the technology can be used to keep the demands of administration under control and to help the teacher to support a child's progress through the curriculum. It is not concerned with new needs such as local financial management (important as that is in the future) or Form 7 (for school statistics), although programs to deal with these are available and better ones will follow.

Such a statement is not as realistic as it may seem, for the programs for one aspect of administration are usually integrated with those that cover others. Data entered for one purpose can be called up and used sensibly in producing information for another without having to re-enter it. Administrative software tends to be a suite of programs dealing with many of the different tasks. Each topic will be discussed separately in the sections that follow, although in practice many of the programs will be found together in one package. The computer too will be referred to as if a separate one is being used for each job, and in some schools this may be so. However, some schools are using a minicomputer to handle all the administrative work, either based in the office or accessible through distributed terminals. There may even be direct links to local education authority offices.

Handling much of this material requires careful security precautions, as several aspects will be sensitive. Many experts encourage the use of encryption techniques to ensure thaï any hacker who gets into the system finds only apparent rubbish, but whether one needs to go that far is debatable. Certainly, however, a password system should be invoked, and teachers should ensure that the words or numbers chosen should not be obviously deducible. 'Maths' as the mathematics department's password is hardly likely to be a barrier to even the most naïve intruder, and yet such a choice has been known! Some levels of information, for example the basic accounting budget of the school, may be further protected by another layer of passwords, and this introduces the concept of people having different levels of privilege to access particular aspects of the information. Some may object to this, but provided the information is accessible in some form it is generally accepted that the right to amend and alter it should be restricted. Organising the computer for administration has to be considered very carefully and there should be sufficient flexibility in the system to allow changes to be made in the light of experience and new developments.

Organising resources

Open learning is assuming considerable popularity, particularly in industrial training, and will obviously find an important place in the repertoire of strategies from which a learner can choose in the future. At the school level, it is represented by supported self-study, the word 'supported' emphasising the need for guidance from a tutor or teacher. Success with this strategy depends on the availability and use of a wide range of resources of all kinds, but access to them requires organisation. Indeed, research-based learning is also dependent on quick access to information and this too means resources.

The term 'resources' covers a wide range of materials - for example books, worksheets, slides, videos, software and artefacts - but it also includes items not usually considered in the same breath: people, factories, woods, and other external sources of information. Recording their accessibility and keeping a track of their use is usually the problem facing the librarian, a person of considerable importance in any school but more especially in those making use of these new systems and strategies. The task of organising resources efficiently is a substantial one, but the technology has facilities that can provide assistance. Nowadays a library without a computer is one suffering from severe deprivation.

The librarian needs to know what is available. A database on a computer is now the easiest way to record this, but it should be a versatile one that produces responses to searches using relatively inaccurate or unclear, often called 'fuzzy', information. Cross-referencing to other related resources would be a normal expectation, and this would include external sources as well as those within the school. Items may be located away from the library itself, for example in a departmental collection, but the existence and accessibility needs to be known centrally. In many schools, the departmental collections are considerable because much of the study through resources takes place in the environment where the expert teachers are. No librarian would query this, but there is a need to ensure that the existence of the resources being used is recorded. Some groups of materials are used in travelling displays, for example to support work on a particular project. While much of these may come from the library itself, others may be on loan from other collections such as the LEA's library or museum service. All need to be recorded and known about if the resources are to be used efficiently.

All this takes time and efficient management. Entering information in the database is a slow process because accuracy is essential. It is, however, more effective for cross-references, and searches should be much quicker. The record also has to be kept up to date. Items are lost and have to be erased; some are moved and this has to be noted; others are added and the records of these have to be included. Sometimes it is possible to download records from a register maintained by the LEA service and this reduces the effort and time spent on that part of the process, but only hard work keeps the database up to date.

The librarian needs an efficient borrow-and-return system. In the public library service, bar codes have proved very popular and successful, and similar systems are available for use in schools. Other electronic markers can be carried by materials which can activate the controls together with a borrower's personal record. The mechanics of these systems ensure more rapid entry into the database than keyboarding and, more important, these systems are more accurate.

Using the computer for this activity provides many advantages. An item located in a search may be identified as out on loan and thus obviate a fruitless hunt for it. Chaser letters can be prepared automatically after due time has elapsed. A record of the use of an item outside the library can be established, and this can affect decisions on stock maintenance.

The computer system is not just a record of borrowers; the program and the data can be used for other information gathering as well – all from one entry as the item passes over the check-out desk.

The librarian needs to know what to purchase. Some information comes from departments and some from the librarian's own ideas. The decision-making chain will differ between schools, but it has to exist and be organised. Information to assist in making the appropriate selection can come from a variety of sources, for example visits from representatives, reviews in the press and journals, recommendations from subject associations, or word of mouth from colleagues in other places. Use should also be made of relevant on-line databases such as Blaise and NERIS, the former the British Library record and the latter the information service of educational materials. 'Books in Print' is available on CD Rom, and a subscription to this will ensure that up-to-date information is present. Having a range of information sources accessible can, in the best-run organisations, encourage their use in determining a sensible purchasing policy for materials.

The librarian then needs to obtain the items selected. Computerised ordering is a developing service, and much time can be saved by ordering through electronic mail from the appropriate suppliers. Part of the record is then already in the database for when the goods arrive. Some materials can be obtained by downloading them from various databases; for example, software can often be obtained from broadcasts or on-line services, and a growing stock of worksheets can be collected this way. Radio and television broadcasts can be recorded from transmissions, recorded automatically through timers or programme location systems. Items may even be sent by facsimile machines. The technology has introduced new methods of obtaining materials, many of which at the same time carry some of the recording information that is needed for the library's stock database. Of course many items will continue to be collected in traditional ways to add to the stock.

The librarian will also be concerned to see that the stock is used effectively. As many items will need the technology to play them, some technical knowledge is necessary. However, the key role is that of supporting children in their learning. Helping them to identify their needs and focus their interest is at the heart of the essential work of all librarians and is the reason why they are so necessary in schools. In addition, though, the new strategies will find the librarian joining the academic staff in providing tutorial support, helping the children to develop their learning processes and skills and sustaining their confidence. There is no need for specialist subject expertise because that is available within the stock or from other teachers, but there is a need to help children to select their methods of learning and thinking and use them efficiently.

The above has been concerned with the materials that make up the school's learning resources, but there is also the collection of equipment which is not necessarily the librarian's responsibility. Stock records of this need to be kept. Equipment which relates directly to particular departments (for example globes) is likely to be recorded by them, but there may be some identified as school resources, such as audiovisual devices and computers. As well as listing their serial numbers etc, it is useful to keep a maintenance record, as this can alert the school to the times when overhaul is needed as well as identifying when replacement is necessary.

Finally, there is maintenance of the stock of consumables within the school. Paper, pencils, discs, cassettes, lamps, folders and ink for duplicators are just some of the essential items that are needed by children, and again the computer can be used to keep track of the rate of consumption to ensure re-ordering at the appropriate time.

The organisation of resources is an essential but often tedious task, the worst aspects of which the technology can help to reduce. Setting up a system needs planning and time, but running it can be easier than other methods and more efficient. A good system reduces the burden on the individual teacher and also increases opportunities for the children to learn effectively.

Records and the curriculum

Pupil records have always been kept by schools, but greater emphasis is being placed on them now with the emergence of profiling as a method of producing a statement of achievement at the end of the school period. Under the regulations of the Data Protection Act care must be taken to allow parental access, but this does not reduce the value of the records. Pupil records are kept satisfactorily on the computer as this provides potential access to all staff quickly, and therefore it is easy to pinpoint and spread essential information about a particular individual.

To maintain an efficient record, the original collection of data has to be undertaken so that entry into the system is simple and accurate. The forms for parents to complete should mirror the layout on the screen if possible as this makes it easier to see that everything is noted. Print-outs for annual checks by parents can be arranged easily and it is then obvious on what part of the screen an alteration has to be made. These records form a sub-set of the general data from which the organisation of the school is developed. Once a record is made, the name at the appropriate level appears in form lists, set lists, option selection files and so on. In a good program suite, there is no need for it to be entered again.

All this, however, is the formality of basic information. The record comes alive when personal academic progress is added. It is easy to cross-reference to these files if a teacher's personal records of a child's progress are held in the same suite of programs, but an alternative is to switch the list of names to a spreadsheet, which can then be the teacher's markbook. A versatile spreadsheet carries verbal as well as numeric information, and can be a useful record of class and individual progress. Selecting different combinations and groups of information for windows to print out can provide relevant material for Parents' Evenings, and graphs of various kinds can be drawn automatically to show the development of a class or an individual.

If a system like supported self-study is adopted, a record of the modules that a child has completed needs to be kept. This will also show areas of difficulty. From this evidence and personal conversations, progress to other modules can be agreed with the child. With the development of appropriate expert systems it is likely that computer evidence can be added to help with the decision making. It is tempting to think that later this will be left entirely to the computer, but there are many reasons to suggest that the human insight of the teacher will be invaluable as the final arbiter with the child. Such progress does need to be recorded, and the computer is ideal for this as it can show matches between what has been completed with various pathways that may be taken next, all at the pressing of a few keys.

Out of this information comes the raw material for the student's profile and achievement records. That for testimonials is also available, and a draft can be held for massaging into an appropriate form for a particular request. Good, accurate profiles are very difficult to create without the background of thorough computerised data, and will take a great deal of time to complete. If the full history of a child is to be taken into account, then use of the database to produce it is very helpful. Paper records are much more difficult to handle.

For children with special needs, statementing is necessary and programs have been written to provide a framework in which this can be done. One of the advantages of this process is that a clear presentation of an individual curriculum is prepared, together of course with notes of progress in achieving it. In order to generate good profiles, a similar procedure could be adopted for the rest of the school population, although prepared in a different way. With supported self-study, notes on module attainments could be used to show progress towards goals agreed between teacher and child, and these would be recorded just like the statements of the special needs child. Another technique is to use profile sentences as signposts of achievement, the word 'profile' here referring to the content to be learned and not the child. Again, recording these on the computer builds up a database that shows a level of progression towards agreed goals which can give a child confidence and security.

These latter examples are introduced to emphasise the interrelationship between the curriculum and the child's record. Using traditional paper systems, the complexity of matching the two and relating them to targets is too much to be practical in reasonable time; on the computer it is very much easier to do, particularly if it is well planned beforehand. From this can emerge the possible establishment of a curriculum designed for an individual child and recorded against that person's progress, the targets being amended and realigned according to the degree of achievement and need that has been agreed. Without the technology, and easy access to it, this would not be possible.

One part of that record will be the projects and assignments that the individual selects to pursue. A criticism of the GCSE has been the amount of such work that a child has to complete, much of it at the same time in March. If the record that all teachers can access were to show the project work in which children were involved and the deadlines to which they were being prepared, then teachers, could help to match and knit their expectations without causing excessive pressure. Some pressure is valuable, but an overdose is potentially dangerous and can lead to under-achievement. This kind of practical curricular use of administrative records can help to make the work of each child more effective.

Options and timetables

When computers first appeared in schools, the first administrative chore for which programs were written was the matter of options. If the power and more especially the size of the memory had been greater, all would have written their timetable programs as well! These are two of the most essential but also most tedious pieces of administrative work, the latter so complex because of the long list of constraints that have to be taken into account. Some subjects must be grouped/not grouped with others because Mr Bloggs teaches them both/they use the same classroom/ there must be time to rearrange it for lunch. We all know the problems.

The difficulty with timetabling is the collection of the data with which the program works. The prevention of clashes whether of subjects, teachers or rooms, and the particular anomalies of an individual school such as the distance between various parts of the campus, mean that the planning of the information and the thoroughness of its collection have to be of a high standard. Once the data are in the computer, the processing and production of the timetable can be done very quickly, and make the sweat, blood and tears that some of us have given to the handmade systems in the past really like a penance. After testing and perhaps introducing corrections, the end result can be issued in various ways. Each teacher can have a personal timetable, as can each room. Departmental timetables, and one that shows the activities of the whole school, can be prepared. More interestingly, a timetable for each individual child can be printed and distributed, listing subject, room and teacher. Form and teaching group lists can be prepared for each teacher, and the program should be able to tell those with access privileges where each child is meant to be at any time of the day.

When linked to other software, all the statutory information required can be collated and prepared. Once pupil record lists are linked to the timetable and staff profiles and availability, most central administrative tasks can be dealt with by relevant cross-referencing. Without the technology, a mass of different collations from paper lists have to be individually prepared and rewritten. If a child moves to another area, either his name is crossed out by hand or the lists where his name appeared are reprinted without it and then distributed as appropriate. The technology has reduced the administrative demands to a more manageable level, at the same time providing detailed information including the work programme of an individual child.

When it comes to fourth-year and sixth-form options, what happens to a particular child becomes more essential. Frequently, the choices are based solely on the ideas of the child and his or her parents, and the opinions of teachers are not registered. Using pupil records, it is easy for a teacher to produce guidance on the levels of achievement which should influence the selection. Information may also be added from any careers analysis that has been taking place, the relevant notes also being on the computer where a program has been assessing the child's interests and matching potential activities to personality. Bringing this information to bear with the child's own choices may lead to more considered views as to which options should be selected. This is not a system for forcing children down a path that they do not want, but for bringing more information to use in reaching agreed decisions.

The options program matches children to subjects and ensures that timetable clashes are reduced to a minimum. From it come print-outs of class lists and timetables. Taking such a process in this way, it is possible to bring an individual into closer personal focus and ensure that a particular child is considered in a unique manner.

Exams and the LEA

At the end of the curriculum are the examinations, at ages 16 and 18. Organising entries has always been a complex administrative exercise, particularly where several examination boards are being used by an individual school. Computers are invaluable in marshalling the data, more especially when linked to pre-existing pupil records. Links to some boards have now been established through electronic mail and the broadcast teletext service, and this can reduce the paperwork involved and permit a school to despatch lists even closer to deadlines. Results too could easily be distributed in this way, and perhaps reduce the time by a few days. Print-outs could then be in a form that suits the school rather than in the motley array of different types of pieces of paper that children receive now.

With the interest in new forms of examination, the accretion of credits against modules for example, the technology could be a considerable asset in ensuring that the evidence was efficiently collected and despatched. By using systems mutually agreed by the boards and the schools, the email service and appropriate use of databases could ensure an accurate and fast service and overcome several of the objections and difficulties that have been raised. The work that children need to do to achieve success could be clarified continually, almost automatically, and much of the anxiety about obtaining the relevant collection of credits could be eliminated. Through continual monitoring by both the board and the school, incipient problems could be eliminated. For adults, knowledge gained through experience is increasingly accepted as credits towards a course and examination, and this same trend should be incorporated in the way in which children manage to get their certificates.

The use of relevant systems of the technology opens out the possibilities for assessment and examination so that children can aim for courses and modules that are more considerate of their individual interests and purposes. If this can be arranged in an acceptable way, it provides the basis for a more flexible and varied approach to the curriculum without reducing the standards that have to be achieved. This has never been possible without the technology as it would require such an increase in resources, especially people, in order that it could be managed efficiently. Now, however, this is more easily accomplished with the computer and direct links to school database systems, but it does need some commitment to put it into place.

The use of computers can encourage the excessive use of assessment points, and care should be taken to ensure that this fast and well-managed service from the technology does not turn the child's programme of study into a nightmare. Geoff Lee (1988), writing in the *Times Educational Supplement*, calculates that

> The South East Graded Assessment in Maths Scheme pictures a grid measuring 11 areas of study by seven levels of achievement, with up to 100 skills in each box for each pupil. Extrapolating this for 1,000 pupils studying 10 subjects, we arrive at 77 million pieces of information.

There is a need for some balance and control!

For the local education authority, there are also gains in communication and links to school data to improve their management and advisory roles. Several now have hard wired computer connections to the school systems within their aegis, while others rely on request and public phone line circuits to transmit messages and obtain the relevant information.

Efficiency has to be matched to the economics, and local email services can make them acceptable substitutes for direct connections. Unlike the civil service no efficient LEA would now rely on exchanges of paper, as these will almost certainly mean rekeying data, with the potential for error, rather than passing it electronically. The target should be similar direct electronic communication to individual teachers.

Many LEAs suffer from difficulties at the sixth-form level with only a few children studying a particular subject in an individual school, and the employment of a teacher just for this is uneconomic. In some places, this situation is aggravated by the shortage of teachers of certain key subjects. Different solutions have been offered – amalgamating sixth forms into a sixth-form college or a total transfer to further education colleges are becoming increasingly common. Some introduce sixth-form clusters, children from several schools meeting at one of them for the relevant subjects so that only one teacher is required. Others are using forms of self-study material, popular in the sciences and mathematics, and this sytem is being expanded into a form of supported self-study with specialist expertise available in the form of county tutors in the problem subjects. Organisation of the cluster system gains in efficiency from good computer databases and efficient communication between the LEA and the schools involved. Without the technology the self-study schemes would be impossible, not just because of management difficulties when pupils are located in several different places but because consultations, delivery, assignments, tutorials and assessments are dependent on it in order that they can take place. Email, telephone conferencing, desk-top publishing, interactive video and similar technical systems are the means by which the materials are provided and the courses are taught. Thus the technology can be valuable in helping LEAs to solve these falling roll/shortage subject problems.

Conclusion

The computer has a more extensive value for administration than has been discussed in this chapter, but these are the aspects that are likely to have the most effect on the curriculum. Teachers are provided with assistance that reduces the burden of the administrative requirements and thus frees them for more time to work with the children. At the same time, information about individual children can be more complete and up to date, so that the help that can be given can be more selective and personal. The curriculum that a child follows can be more uniquely tailored to fit individual requirements and may even be designed separately for each child. With the facility to record and monitor this reasonably closely, new ways can be used to present the elements of the curriculum, encouraging greater participation by the child and therefore supporting the trend towards greater autonomy.

This depends on resources, and through programs on the computer their management and control can be improved so that they can be used more effectively. To be successful, such changes to the curriculum also require more flexibility in the examination system but the practical problems associated with this can be eased through the technology as well. When the child leaves school, administrative programs are available to ensure that a good profile can be produced and appropriate references and testimonials written without too much effort.

All these positive gains are within reach, provided appropriate equipment and software are purchased in sufficient quantities and distributed sensibly. The technology is there to reduce the chores that come with administrative demands and to give teachers the opportunity to concentrate on their work with children. Yet, there are dangers that go along with so much dependence on the technology. Computers are only right if the program is correctly written and the data that are fed in are accurate. Too much reliance can lead to inflexibility. No program has yet been written that takes account of all the variations in human behaviour and physical adequacy, nor is one likely to appear for many years to come. The experience and sensitivity of an understanding teacher is needed to interpret and intervene, and to ensure that the peculiarities of each individual are taken into account, not just in general but also at certain times. A good teacher does this in a way that nurtures and supports a child's learning, and the cold print-outs of the computer must be used with sufficient flexibility to allow for it. In a dispute with the computer, the good teacher is likely to have a better understanding of the child.

Another danger is that pressure will be placed on a child to learn faster and achieve more because the computer says that progress through the curriculum is too slow. Some pressure is valuable, and some children gain from being stretched. Others respond by freezing their interest or dropping standards. Again, the good teacher knows and recognises the signs, while the computer, using the programs that are likely over the next decades, will not respond.

Thus, while there are great advantages for the curriculum in using the technology in administrative matters a balance has to be kept, and human monitoring and intervention should be encouraged and accepted where it is necessary. Starting these programs requires time, planning and labour but, when they are working, greater freedom for teacher and child is possible.

References

Lee, G (1988) Strategic View: The Main Considerations for Schools and LEAs *Times Educational Supplement* 11. 3. 88, p.65, London

Part 3

Implications for Tomorrow's Curriculum

Chapter 5

The Needs of Society

Introduction

Education is part of the pattern of society. While it may be interesting and pleasing for those involved to think of it as something separate, it is intertwined with changes of thinking and the needs of society. Children grow up into society, not into a limbo of education, and have to participate, develop and recreate it. Their new definitions become the new shape of society, and their activities generate its wealth and culture. The mess they find is their parents', and the mess they leave behind is theirs. The theme of this part of the book is to argue for a new look at education because there is a new look to society. This has not arisen for any political or economic reasons, although they have a continuing influence, but because of the technologies which have been developed and which affect the potential and behaviour of humanity. The principal technology that is creating this change is that based around the microprocessor – so-called information technology – but the impact of biotechnology and that associated with materials is also substantial and will be accommodated in some of the comments made.

Writing on such a large canvas as the changes in society inevitably depends on generalisations, some very sweeping, but space is limited and the purpose is to provide sufficient background to draw some early feelers for the direction in which education should be going. As with all generalisations, there are exceptions and oddities that are swept under the carpet and ignored but in a larger space would be covered or explained. Using them to invalidate the generalisations is to be over-concerned about the stray elm when we are trying to sort direction and purpose from the large forest of conifers in which it grows. The elm will be important, but at a later time.

Stonier (1983) has described three societies: agricultural, industrial and information, and in his view it is the last into which we are proceeding at a great pace. For Alvin Toffler (1980), this is the third wave, with many differences from the previous two but an inevitable consequence of them. To Daniel Bell (1973), this is the post-industrial society, dependent on its past but of a different character. Three very different people, they come to very similar conclusions. The characteristics may vary in tone and intensity, but the general tenor is agreed.

It would be comforting to believe that the new society is just a development of the old, slightly different but requiring no drastic changes – the old, perhaps, in new clothes. Feed in the same basics, for the inner child is the same even if the outer behaviour tangles with these new-fangled computers. Comforting, but is it true? Of course, there is some reality to this, for humans have not changed nor are about to change dramatically. Medicine will provide more genetic control over offspring, but fundamentally they are the same biological entities. Society does not suddenly stop and then a new form instantly emerge, but there is an apparently seamless evolution from the one to the other. Thus, much of the shape of the future is laid down in the form of the present – the same emotions, similar games, reflections of much of the same technologies. Hindsight can describe remarkable differences, foresight can envisage them, but present sight sees only the same issues and problems.

Education, however, is properly concerned with foresight, for the outputs from its work use their investment many years after the first premium has been accepted. The value of the curriculum for the four-year-old in 1988 is not seen in society at large until at least the year 2000, and the question must be whether it will be worth anything. Today's curriculum is grounded within a clerical/verbal tradition where the nuances and record of words play an essential role in agreement and interpretation. Visual evidence is of less value, as is technical and scientific unless it is rewritten in words. The basis for this is the paper record, the databank of the past and the precedents on which the present is understood. Databank records are very different now, and while we still tinker with words because of tradition, the picture, holograph, video and three-dimensional model are often more accurate and more expressive, and all now form part of the same databank. Much of this has been possible before, but the power of tradition has not allowed it to emerge with sufficient vigour. This society believes credibility is given to a document that has been inscribed with a signature, even when that has been created by a rubber stamp.

The curriculum is still designed to facilitate entrance to higher education, and thus it is heavily governed by the necessary requirements. Content and teaching are geared to this, and success is recognised as entry to university or polytechnic. Academically the rest have failed, although various standards may have been achieved that demonstrate to future employers the merits of the pupil. Because teachers have frequently come from an academic environment, specialised in a particular subject, there is a satisfaction and pleasure in helping children to understand and develop a similar interest in it. Even at a lesser level of attainment than passing to higher education, there is satisfaction in seeing children gain knowledge and interest in the fascination of a particular specialist subject, for the subject itself is seen to be of value.

Some subjects carry more status than others. Science was once a poor relation, but in the 1960s it became more acceptable. Technology, home economics and practical subjects tend to be of lesser status, perhaps because they do not feature highly in the spectrum of studies at higher education establishments. Gaining respectability for a new subject in higher education requires that it has academic rigour, a curiously ill-defined quality which academics in general feel is present. Usually, the way to obtain this is to include the 'history and philosophy' of the subject!

For the 80 per cent who fail to achieve entrance to higher education the subjects have still been taught in the same way, although some have had variations and simplifications of the various syllabuses. Where possible, practical subjects have been included, but the emphasis has been on ensuring that they fit into some of the basic requirements for general jobs. In the last few years this has not been so apparent, but in the 1950s to 1970s the feeling that children were being prepared for the conveyor belt was strong. This matched the demand for discipline, because ill-discipline on the production line was inefficient and expensive. Apprenticeships were important targets when they were more prevalent – long-winded and tedious as many of them were, they led to jobs for life with a company.

This could be described as the industrial curriculum, preparing people in the same way through very set and organised timetables on roughly the same content to emerge at the end as grades of quality. The highest level went to higher education, the next lower to offices and under-management, the next to apprenticeships and trade, and the lowest to support the infrastructure. The criterion for the grades was the level of achievement in verbal and memory tests, although at the lower levels some practical products could be included in the judgement. Education was then over, except for those in the top group who went to higher tiers.

For many, probably the majority, school was a bad time. Some people and teachers were nice and some memories of the social relationships were pleasurable, but the structure, work pattern and curriculum were unpleasant, boring or irrelevant. Factory life started at a very young age, even if it was called school. Choice and personal control of one's life were limited, and many children came and went almost unnoticed. Teachers were aware of the good and the bad, but average children progressed 'satisfactorily' as entries in a markbook. Most of the content was irrelevant; if one was not going to be a chemist, why study chemistry? English was useful in order to read and write, but who was going to use words like clause, metaphor, hyperbole or synonym in the future as they loaded boats in the docks or managed check-out staff in the supermarket? Education was needed to get a job, they said, but for most of the jobs it was clear that the education received was of very little value.

Within the clerical/verbal tradition, perhaps most obvious now in the civil service where even being good at maths is slightly suspect, these topics and subjects were seen as important. In truth to some degree they were, for if one was ever to progress in later life these were part of the knowledge that was needed to do it. But they were the cause of much disenchantment with education as an activity. I learned Latin and have found it useful since, particularly in helping to understand English. The phrase was: 'Latin helped to train your mind', and it certainly is useful in dealing with language structures and logic. However, it is typical of the clerical/verbal tradition that these are very high prerequisites for a good mind.

The other characteristic of the so-called industrial curriculum is that all children, arranged in classes, progress at about the same rate through the same material. This is apparently an economic way to approach teaching, but it takes no account of personal variations in attitude, pace of uptake, mode of learning, or order of acceptance. If the teacher's chosen method is not acceptable, failure results or the child lags behind.

With the appearance of the GCSE some of these issues are being overcome, but others persist. The subjects remain the same, as does much of the content, although the weight of factual memorisation has been reduced substantially. Through the use of continual assessment, pacing is not so rigorous; however, the classes are still taught in the same way without necessary regard for individual variation. Behind the curriculum, and behind the preparatory writings on the national curriculum that is to follow, the same ethos of the clerical/verbal tradition remains.

Making judgements now is difficult, for we are in transition between the industrial society and the next, which I shall call the 'information society'. Times of transition are always difficult because the future may be clear in general, but it is unclear in detail and that is how it impinges on individuals and is judged by them. It is like moving house, when the dimensions of the new one are known but the siting of plugs and taps has not been noted. This can make all the difference to the position of the furniture and indeed how much of it can be taken.

Transition also leads to conflicts that can become very bitter. A new place may be the occasion to resurrect all the older values that have been weakened or discarded, a 'return to the basics' as they are usually referred to in education, but they may have disappeared because they did not help children to succeed in society. The past is always flavoured with romanticism which belies the truth, and is treasured by those who succeeded because they believe it helped them to get where they are. For the vast number who failed, however, the view is different – one which did not help them succeed, and indeed consigned them to the 'also rans' of society. Working harder was no solution because the methods and goals did not necessarily match theirs, and blaming the teachers is to ignore the system they were employed to expound.

During transition these arguments come and go, whether they refer to education or the decline of personal relations with the customer in shops and banks. In the past, the middle class tradition was to pay one's way and owe nothing, but now industry, commerce and domestic life rely on credit or, as the great Northern commedian Bobby Thompson described it, 'the debt'. Transition is the time when these debates take place, and for the curriculum – which must be looking to the future – it is particularly difficult to maintain a balance when future needs are not clear. Traditions are valuable and they provide an underlying theme for civilised life but they have to change, adapt and perhaps be discarded if they are no longer beneficial or an apt prescription. In a different world we have to start from the beginning again, use our history and culture to guide us, but come to new conclusions that are more appropriate.

And the beginning in education is its aims. Eric Bolton (1987), the Senior Chief Inspector of HMI at the Department of Education and Science lists them as:

> to satisfy the developing educational needs of individual pupils and students; to prepare young people for active, informed citizenship; to equip young people with the skills and understanding they need to earn a living and to live productive lives.

There may be variations in wording; for example, I find the word 'satisfy' too finite in the first aim, but in general they cover what education is about. The difficult issue is the context in which the citizenship and productive life will be exercised, the shape of society. It is to draw a generalised picture of that with which the next section is concerned. Many books have been written on this subject, and the picture described is a personal interpretation of the views of many authors including Daniel Bell (1973), Christopher Evans (1979), Tom Stonier (1983), James Martin (1978), Ian Barron (1979), Peter Large (1980), Jenkins and Sherman (1979), Alvin Toffler (1980), Nora and Minc (1980), Burkitt and Williams (1980), Jacques Vallee (1984)) and NEDO (1987).

The character of tomorrow's society

It is called the information society, because it is dominated by information. Data may be used by intelligent machines to create products or to monitor and control the environment, or be used by people to generate further information, provide insight and entertainment, and produce new materials, products and resources. To harness all this information, society is very dependent on technology of all kinds.

Houses will be 'intelligent' – that is, they will respond to the movement of human beings, changing light and temperature as needed, having total internal communication systems to every room with remote control of all facilities such as cooking, taps in baths, record players and so on. All storage areas will be linked to databases, so as products move in and out of the freezer, for example, they are added or subtracted from the totals. Lists for purchasing will be generated by the difference between an established norm and what is present on the database, as well as personal additions. Security will respond to the recognition of known and unknown people. The controls will be addressable remotely and may even be observed from afar, so that the 'house' is warned of arrivals. All the controls will have the facility to be alterable and overriden by human intervention, so if one wants a room to remain cold and dark one day, it can be ordered that way. Materials will be designed for cleanliness and change, so that items can be adjusted for space and surfaces easily altered to create different environments. The aim will be to support individuality and flexibility. While remote areas will be dependent on satellite connections, the wired village and town will be the norm. Much of the information made available through these wires will be entertainment, but interactive connections to data centres – the local information service – will be a significant part of the provision. Home collections of material will continue to develop, even though access to public information will be easier than today. Electronic mail will be a normal mechanism for communication, and many people will have fax available as well.

The home will be the workplace for many, providing either office-type facilities or the setting for garden-shed industries. Communication facilities will mean that a great deal of the activities that many people now associate with offices will be undertaken in the home instead: project management, draughting work, journalism, law and accountancy are examples. Information required will be downloaded as needed, collaboration with colleagues being effected by seeing and discussing each other's work shared electronically and involving people in all parts of the country and world. Garden-shed industries will be specialised in the mass production of small items or the preparation of items tailored to particular purposes with limited customers.

While much contact between people will be through electronic services or within the local community, travel will bring together working groups for occasional meetings to develop relationships. This will be for business and commercial purposes, but there will also be much travel to visit places and people, explored second-hand through the various information sources. By concentrating so much activity within the local community, there will be a desire to visit other places. Improvements in travel facilities will make this faster and easier with more built-in guidance systems.

Industry will depend heavily on automation, but using systems that respond to individualising products to meet particular requests. Thus modular construction will be popular to support interchangeability where possible. People will be needed to monitor more than construct in many factories, the emphasis being on quality control and testing. Others will provide high-level technical and engineering skills to improve efficiency and introduce modifications, for design and development of variations to a product will also be important. Cleaning, sorting, and some warehousing will remain in the hands of people, as will maintenance of the plant. Employment of large numbers of people in a production industry will be rare and constantly threatened with redundancy.

Structurally, there will be a growth of international holding companies responsible for large numbers of self-directed small companies. Prototypes of new products will be developed by small specialist groups – some a part of these companies, others independent. Such work will be ideal for garden-shed industries. Manufacture will be done by companies that specialise in this, like fulfilment agencies, able to rearrange their plant for different products. It will appear that all factories will be producers of items designed and prototyped elsewhere, and they may be independent or part of a larger organisation. Changes to products will be programmed into the system from instructions prepared by the design groups.

With changes to products, programmes and personnel, there will be a substantial need for training and retraining to keep staff up to date and able to deal with new developments. This will be particularly important for those involved in marketing and selling the products. People will also move between the various companies in a multinational group, sharing skills and procedures, and this will be one mechanism for training.

Service and leisure industries will be substantial, but automated as far as possible. Thus financial exchanges will be made by cards, which will either debit directly or, in the case of transport, at the end of a journey, or will debit a credit agency and then be charged to a person's account at an agreed level. Cash will not be used very much. Leisure facilities will be a major feature of all towns, bookable through the local information service, and great emphasis will be placed on their value.

Jobs in these service industries will concentrate on general management of the various systems: consultants, many of whom will operate independently, to interpret the systems to people; assistants who will welcome, serve and guide people through transactions or activities. Some shops will be automated, as in supermarkets, but others, like the cake shop, will be personalised with assistants. Where it is possible offices will be abolished, as much of the work will be done by machine or at home. Some buildings will specialise as 'meeting places' and be booked for that purpose, supplied with appropriate facilities. Most of the activities in the gambling dens of the stock market will be carried out remotely and the city buildings will become largely vacant.

Many activities of the law and accountants will be executed by individuals themselves, dealing with expert system programs. Resort to human experts will take place when any party is unable to agree or there is doubt raised by the computer. Thus, usually automatic trivia such as wills, divorce, house purchase and VAT returns will normally be done through the system, but criminal charges or disputes over allowances will be dependent on human intervention. Medicine and health care will remain largely undertaken by human expertise, heavily supported by technology. Many congenital problems will be overcome through genetic engineering, and treatment will be targeted more towards particular tissues or disease causing organisms. Flexibility of treatment will be important, and more will be given at home supported by visiting health staff. Hospitals will be places for highly technical treatment and instant care after accidents. Most people will recuperate at home, monitored through the information network to which various parameters can be sensed and related. Much attention will be given in hospital to those needing rest and recuperation, developed by paramedical staff. Personal health monitoring will be a feature available for people to use, mostly undertaken by automatic measuring systems.

Home health care staff will be part of the essential infrastructure of society. People will be employed to use machinery to support the basic systems of roads, water, power, information network, as well as the police, fire and information services, and so on. So dependent will society be on the efficiency of the technology that a citizens' technology advice bureau may be established with teams of specialist staff able to visit homes or ensure that repairs are made. Maintenance will be a significant characteristic of society, and people will be employed purely to ensure that essential public systems are constantly in order.

The garden-shed industries mentioned earlier are just one feature of the trend towards a multiplicity of small businesses, many of them geared towards producing unique objects as in old crafts such as woodworking or for particular firms, supporting domestic or community requirements such as plumbing or window replacements or developing prototypes for exploitation elsewhere. One business will be the supply of support services to the home office worker, sometimes full-time but more usually on a part-time or occasional basis.

It would be wrong to get the impression of stability in this picture of different types of work. The rule will be flexibility and change, partly because the people involved will wish to do something different but also because the demand for different activities will fluctuate. For stability of employment, medical and infrastructure jobs are good choices, but they will be subject to constant change as the technology develops and people working in this field will have to be as amenable to flexible practices and retraining as in any other.

Life will be based on communities, relatively small in each case. Any individual will belong to a variety of them, for example that where the house is, that associated with a club or church, that linked to work which may include people all over this country and others, that developed through multimedia correspondence which will be worldwide. The more these overlap, the greater the personal sense of security. Because much work will be based in the house, home and work communities will have many common elements; where commuting, which will be much reduced, persists, effort may have to be made to make them cross each other.

Cities will decline in importance, and tend to split more into separate 'small towns' – communities for living. The role of cities will be centres of leisure activities, including shopping which will be increasingly on the hypermarket design, transport junctions and major services. Most will be 'wired', as will communities for business, information and entertainment purposes. A few offices will exist, as well as meeting room complexes and hotels. Cities, as opposed to the 'towns', will not be places for living, and factories will be placed nearer to living communities. There will be a significant movement towards caring for the environment around living communities, and the quality of life will depend on the relationship between the facilities of the living community and its surrounding countryside.

Communities will be determined to ensure a self-sustaining environment: local shops, information facilities, factories, access to entertainment features, and a range of trades, crafts and skills that will maintain the life. Greater status will be given to those responsible for maintaining the community and its infrastructure, and personal knowledge of the people will grow in order to ensure a balance of contribution to its success. Education and training facilities will be a community asset of importance, for the knowledge value added to people in the community will enhance its position and success. The role of the communities will dominate social decision making, and together with the multinational companies will form a major political force. Indeed, industry and communities will work much closer together than at present. The information service will be sufficiently powerful and effective to provide a less important central government with all the data for national decisions, and the civil service will be substantially reduced and less significant.

Social attitudes will be based around the well-being of the family – not necessarily the standard nuclear arrangement – and the community. Because paid employment will come and go, there will be a need for a more entrepreneurial attitude to seek out ideas for wealth creation and develop them. Much of this will rest on the judicious use of needs elicited from the information service, and the requirements of the community. Life will appear more comfortable, and much effort will be given to finding physical and mental challenges and adventurous activities. Electronics will play a substantial part in the do-it-yourself interest, and the jokes will not be about fuses but about mending glass fibres and soldering. Indeed, do-it-yourself enthusiasm will grow and a substantial part of personal time will be spent in such activities, both for an individual's own environment and for that of other members of a local community. The range of activities will be extensive and certainly not limited to carpentry, painting and plumbing.

Unpaid time will be spent in leisure pursuits of a wide and expanding range. There will be 'groups' of interest in many things, and the lack of fellow enthusiasts in the community will be compensated for by easier worldwide connections to people with a similar bent. Such communications will not only be verbal; much use will be made of visual and three-dimensional descriptions. Many of these leisure pursuits will involve the family as the dominant feature of much of the perspective on life.

People will move from one community to another, sometimes for reasons of work, but much less so than in the past as so much can be done from the home base. The weekend cottage syndrome will not be popular as the contribution to the community will not be easily sustained, but it will not be as necessary anyway in this form of society. By contributing to the community and adding to its knowledge and skill base, the community itself will become more active and prosperous. The added values of information, leading to imagination and invention, will be the core of wealth, but the community will gain as the country and perhaps the world does as well. Communities without a close sense of allegiance will not provide the necessary support and may fail.

The paradox is the growing importance of the individual. For many people, the appearance of the computer seems to have turned them all into numbers, which indeed it has, and this suggests anonymity. The information society will have the other effect; the views, needs and identity of each number will become more important and the personalisation of products of all kinds will become easier to achieve. Thus, in this society, the individual will become more noticeable and important, and each person's views more recognised. Communication facilities will make it easier to pass questions and ideas to those with responsibilities for decision making, and contributions to debates on public issues will not be limited by having to be at a certain place at particular times.

The range of skills within communities will be wide. Forecasting manpower needs is already difficult, and will become increasingly so. People will change their special interests and activities throughout their life. This will be for many reasons – boredom, a new interest, new needs for skills, suggestions to work with friends, missing skills within the community, and others. The key will be flexibility, adapting to new circumstances and retraining as needed. However, the dependence on the use of technology will be high, so technological skills will be expected in everybody.

The issues and problems that will confront society will be as varied and changeable as they are now. One problem will be constantly significant, however, and that is the balance between commitment to the community and the desire to be anonymous, private and separate. While much effort will be made to ensure that records of individuals' transactions are kept in separate packages that are not interconnected, the person who wishes to opt out altogether will have difficulties. The survival and role of the dissident will be the subject of continuing debate.

The speed with which the information society will appear is not uniform. Some elements are already in place while others are a long way off. Some will depend on investment policies whereas the speed of development of others will relate to political decisions. By the year 2000 a great deal will be present, although changes will continue to occur and shape the structures. Indeed, change will characterise the information society which will gain its own stability within a context of flexibility. Because it will encourage and depend on invention and development, new products and attitudes will be appearing constantly and will have to be absorbed into the structure and behaviour.

However, even those who find such a society unpleasant will find it very difficult to stop it emerging. There is an inevitability about it which political and financial decisions can only defer, not stop. Those reaching it fastest will influence the design and relationships elsewhere, while those trying to wait and see will find its structures gradually imposed. While my concern here is to do with the influence of the technology, there are many other social factors encouraging the development of the society, although the technical effects are a considerable driving force. The picture in the preceding paragraphs is necessarily broad and in many places faint, for to go into further detail would be to lead away from the educational theme. From the foregoing, it is possible to extract an initial description of the general educational needs, and that is the purpose of the next section.

The needs of tomorrow's people

Just as the description of the information society takes a broad approach, so this section does not attempt to draw in too many details. From the following general description of needs, a later chapter will begin to create the parameters for a curriculum to meet them. The difference between the present and the future is considerable, even though some of the groundwork is already beginning to appear.

Perhaps the key word to the information society is flexibility. Change will be taking place all the time, and people will need to adjust and adapt to it. Uncertainty is a major feature, for many of the old reliable continua such as long-term employment will have disappeared for most people. Change also means the need to adapt enthusiasms to fit into new patterns of interests and opportunities for paid activities.

Uncertainty leads to lack of confidence and difficulty in maintaining a self-image, particularly in times of real as opposed to potential trouble. Some support can come from other members of the community, so individuals will help to build each other up and sustain enthusiasm. From the community can come a sense of being wanted, of importance, but a sense of purposefulness and commitment must come from inside the individual. If people believe in their capabilities and have a sense of internal direction, some measure of self-confidence develops. Combined with the support of the community, and of course members of a family, this gives strength to endure times of unpaid living and uncertainty, and also the drive to learn new skills. Thus a major requirement of personal development is the acquisition of confidence and self-conviction.

Some will find help in spiritual and philosophical searches and experiences. For many people, the strength of religious belief sustains their confidence and gives them a rationale for living. Others look for a broader philosophical stance against which to judge their actions, but the exploration and development of insights and beliefs like these can form additional support. At times when emotions are raw, using a balanced spiritual or philosophical outlook can introduce a method of coping and creating a positive outlook.

The importance of confidence is that it carries the individual through difficulties that come with flexibility. It helps to motivate and drive the commitment to retraining or developing new interests, to approach new possibilities, to attempt what has not been tackled before. Being flexible requires that courage which chances a new approach or a new venture, and does not depend on being cossetted in an everlasting rut. Such daring is developed from understanding one's capabilities and perhaps chancing a little more, for with that knowledge is the confidence to try. All personal development should be seeking to encourage people to appreciate these possibilities within themselves.

To meet some of the changes, an entrepreneurial attitude will be beneficial. Self-confidence gives individuals the strength to go out and sell their abilities and ideas, not always for money in the information society where its significance will be less, but also within the community. It needs an imaginative and enquiring approach to the world to identify opportunities, an analytical outlook to measure their potential and the drive to exploit them. Being inventive and even noticing a need is only half the skill; equally important is the management of the structures and relationships that help one obtain any needed support and develop the niche that has been identified.

This attitude is fostered by the general environment, in this case the community, but is also developed through the methods of education. It is not necessarily competitive, although in some instances that is helpful, but it does require a certain amount of decision-making skills backed by good analysis. Imagination and curiosity are probably more important, as each member of a partnership can add much to the others. It is as important to have the entrepreneurial skill to offer to paint fences within the local community as it is to develop and produce a new engine. Noticing a need, recognising that one can fill it and how it is to be done are at the heart of the process.

In this technological society, being comfortable with all the devices and systems as well as having the confidence to use them are essential requirements. The technology will naturally keep changing and developing, but these new forms should breed excitement and interest, not anxiety. People should be looking for new opportunities and uses that can be exploited from them, savings in efficiency and the gains in control over the environment. When microcomputers appeared there were many who boasted how little they knew about them or were interested in them, but this is not acceptable in the information society. Just as the illiterate today are those who do not understand the general principles of computers, so the illiterate in the information society will be those who do not have a grasp of the concepts behind the technology they are using. The home, the environment, industry and entertainment will be dependent on it, and people will need to know the principles on which it works. Some will take that interest further, and there will be a number of levels of expertise ranging from professionals through technicians to gifted amateurs with their do-it-yourself skills. Those in the last category will need to comprise a substantial part of the population, and therefore much training will be needed.

Being able to accept a piece of technology and then use all its facilities will depend on the effective use of guides and manuals, a recognition of the basic concepts and an inherent confidence. Most people will need to be able to do general maintenance of their equipment, fit it into the circuitry of their homes and program it as necessary to match their habits. That will be part of ordinary living. There will be people requiring different levels of training and specialisation to take on a range of work, and as this is unlikely to remain stable, most will have periods of retraining to adjust their knowledge to new developments or uses. Employment may be in industry, in the infrastructure of society, or in the design of new products or prototypes. Some of these will be part of the garden-shed enterprises.

Knowledge of the concepts behind technology will lead to more informed decision making when purchases are being planned at all levels. Many companies bought the wrong computers because directors lacked the education and knowledge to understand what was being offered, but in the information society the level of knowledge must be such to ensure that investment in the technology is based on understanding. The same applies at all levels of purchasing. Such knowledge is also important in ensuring that decision makers have views founded on at least a general understanding of the technical problems on which they are working. In the information society, ignorance will be at a lower general level than now, and decisions will be taken more professionally than is frequently the case at present.

Information will be readily accessible from all over the world in large quantities. Through wired environments, decisions will be made based on information, and data will also be transferred rapidly between homes, information centres, services, trading sites, factories and all the other aspects of the community. People will need to know how to access this, including the use of the technology, but more important they will need to know how to handle and use it. A requirement for data or information will be made into the system, but there will be several potential sources of answers and some choices will have to be made, cost being one significant criterion. Usually much more than is necessary will be supplied, and this will require selection, sorting, mixing with other information, the quality weighed, and the knowledge gained used in some way. None of this comes naturally from some genetic control, although maybe even that will come about in the future! It develops from education and practice, from errors as well as successes.

Being able to gather and organise information is also crucial to developing interests. When there is more unpaid time, there is greater opportunity to expand and explore ideas and happenings that arouse interest. Time can be spent in diversions and entertainment, and indeed such activities are often important in enriching and stimulating thinking and planning. However, time can also be used creatively when curiosity stirs up enthusiasm to investigate a topic and get interested in it. Topics need not be limited to stamp collecting or music making, but can be as varied and open as possible. Just as fundamental scientific research is concerned with subjects that excite individual scientists, so interests should be in those areas which stimulate rather than necessarily appear practical and useful. It is surprising how many of these can emerge as socially valuable activities.

Fundamental to success in all parts of this new society is skill in information handling and use. Most activities will be dependent on it, and the added value from information of all kinds will be responsible for progress. But the information itself will be of little use unless it is communicated to other people. Much time will be spent in communication using a variety of mechanisms - some artistic, some literary, some oral. Video, for example, will be an important mechanism as will the use of a range of computer programs, not just wordprocessors. Audiocassettes are already a means of promoting products (including presidential candidates in America), being passed through the door like political leaflets, and they are just part of the broadening range of methods of communication.

While much will be within the local community, the increase in international conversation by electronic means will be considerable. People in different countries will be considered to be next-door neighbours as they share in conversations and discussions undertaken through email and conferences. Satellites and cable will bring news, views and entertainment from all over the world, and the potential for dialogue and understanding between nations will be considerable. The importance of understanding and using foreign languages will rise, but much dialogue will take place in only one language.

Communication requires skills and attitudes that need to be developed and updated. There are technical elements but the majority of the issues relate to 'language', whether that is a foreign tongue or the visual relationships in a video. Understanding and producing graphical displays will be part of the dialogue between people, but this comes from guidance on interpretation and use and is not an instinctive response. In the information society, the role of communication will assume more importance because the mechanisms will be so flexible and widespread. However, this is not about one 'language' but a range of different ones, and thus communication must be considered in terms of a spread of different facilities and versatile systems.

From good communication comes collaboration and co-operative work. While there will be a place for the individual acting in isolation, the information society will operate around interdependence between people. Communication systems encourage this and ease some of the problems, although only people reduce the interpersonal difficulties that inevitably arise. The communities are based on collaboration and mutual support, and working practices will be similarly dependent on co-operation. Much of this will take place at a distance, again using the various technical mechanisms available. Specialists, for example in the law, will work in collaboration rather than mark their independence. There will be a need to realise the importance of these interrelationships, and to learn to overcome many of the prejudices and difficulties that occur between people. Racism and sexism are current examples, but there will be others that emerge in the context of society itself. Travel will assist in overcoming some prejudices but this will be brought about from living and sharing within the community being visited rather than imposing an alien community upon it. Much of the present holidaying process by the British in Spain is this pseudo-colonial imposition of behaviour patterns, so that the food, drinking and leisure attitudes are those of the British rather than the Spanish. Collaborative attitudes are opposed to this, the visiting community needing to meld its behaviour within the mores of that being visited. Part of the value of international dialogue will be the promotion of this understanding, but it will also need to evolve as part of people's insight into personal relationships.

Another aspect of collaboration will relate to the local environment. The technological capacity to monitor and even control the environment means that there is more information about its state and needs, but responding to that raises difficulties over the balance between exploitation for human purposes and conservation of quality. Living with a good environment is itself a form of collaboration, but the issue here relates to the need to support an appropriate balance between the demands placed upon it. Because the level of information will be greater, and the ability to monitor the effects more accurate and complete, those debating the use will be more aware of the state of the environment and the consequences of actions. The community will have a responsibility for its environment and for ensuring the sustenance of a vibrant and healthy ecology, but the decisions to bring this about will be difficult.

Participation in this debate is one part of the personal civic responsibilities of all members of the community. The availability of information and the speed of communications theoretically makes it easier to be informed about the data on which decisions will be made. However, the issues will remain complex and for many people will require interpretation, which instantly means the introduction of personal views. Several people have suggested that information technology will improve the democratic process of society because information will be more readily available, but this is only true if time and effort can be spent on sorting and analysing it. We may not be so dependent on collecting press cuttings of data, which will be instantly available on line, but we will need just as much time, if not more, to analyse the data and draw appropriate democratic conclusions. Thus other people's interpretations will remain the guide for many, and their persuasiveness and assumed prejudices will be the reason for supporting a particular decision. As with all information – and someone's interpretation is as much information as the original data – the responsibility of the user is to test its validity and weigh its value.

Participation in democracy is a necessary part of citizenship, but understanding how to find data and weigh up issues and arguments is part of the expertise that individuals have to acquire. Within a community every view is seen to count, and the same must apply in the broader layers of decision making at national and international stages. Where data and professional interpretation are at present ignored by amateur administrators, the weight of community and individual views will have to be used to produce more sensitive and wiser decisions.

Industry too will have a closer relationship with the communities in which it is based. As holding companies become more international, allegiances will become more local. Again this appears to be a paradox, but it is a logical consequence of improved communications and the nature of the 'global village' concept. Good local relationships are important for those who work for the industry, for the many who service them and the manufacturing base itself. An industry that fails to foster these relationships loses its local influence and its development base. New ideas will emerge as much from the community as from the industry itself, and where it is an appropriate fulfilment operation it will gain from the prototype development of the local people, as of course will any holding company with its international outlook.

The progress and demands of industry will be reflected in retraining within the community, and there will be a close relationship between it and general educational activity.

While this appears to refer only to major industries within an area (that is, those with international connections), it will also be true for all who are involved in industrial and commercial practice within a community, whether they are shop workers, medical personnel or garden-shed workers. These are also contributors to the productive and development work of the community, and have as much interest in its success and liveliness as those with wider connections. Their participation is as valuable and will be part of the contributions to the viability of the community's life. They too will support the educational activity, and they too will benefit from the added value that comes from it. In a collaborative society, all those responsible for its wealth have a contribution to make to it as well as draw from it.

Those involved in paid work, as well as those without it, need leisure and cultural facilities through which to give balance and insight to their perceptions. Such facilities are provided through the community, sometimes relayed or direct from national and international sources, sometimes strictly local in origin. Participation may come easily like listening to popular music, or require a degree of training like acting in a play. Some may be conducted at an elementary level like participating in a beetle drive, or at a more sophisticated level like playing in a chess tournament. The range of provision and accessibility will be wide, but to delve deeper into a facility or reap more insight and sensitivity from it requires a background of training or education. What the community provides will be a measure of the desire of the participants, but all communities will be seeking to offer opportunities for more sophistication and deeper experiences. Participation includes being part of an audience but it emphasises joining in the creation as well, and this requires confidence, interest, attitudes and skills.

Other important parts of leisure are health activities – participation in sport interpreted in its widest sense. Walking in the environment is as much part of this as being a member of the local football team. Health activities will usually be based on facilities provided by the community, and these will tend to be increasingly extensive and varied. As wide a range of opportunities as possible will be offered to members of the community so that an array of tastes and interests can be accommodated. Only through the possibility of sampling will individuals find what suits them best, and education will encourage such opportunities to be taken. Again, the word is participation, for the joining in – at whatever is suitable for the age as well as the abilities of the individual – is a contribution to the community. The walker who is crossing the fells alone is contributing, as is the squash player who always loses.

Reading this may have produced a feeling of an avuncular community, all-seeing and all-demanding. Participate, support, work with your community or be ostracised, may be the impression that is emerging. To some degree this is true, for the interdependent, collaborative ethos of the community will be strong. It will thrive on the added value provided by those who join in, and lose when they move away. It will work with other communities on joint ventures, such as the Resource Software house in Doncaster, exploiting its talents and industry nationally and internationally. It will gain at all levels from information and communication structures that will be available. Its strength however will be its people, and their participation will be its character. To that extent, it will be demanding.

Opting out will be difficult because using the facilities of the community without participating will not be welcomed. Paying for them with money will not be the same as the added value from talent and ability. This will be a major social issue for the information society. Through the technology, individuals will be well known and society will be clearly less private than appears to be the case now. Most of the information that will be known is available, but only with difficulty and searching. In the information society, that same data will be accessible at high speed and with greater convenience. Opting out into anonymity will therefore be more difficult.

For certain groups, for example the caring professions, the problems of privacy have been of concern for a long time; because of the technology, preserving a proper sense of secrecy will be made more difficult. Nonetheless, this is part of the professionalism of the job and will be sustained. Indeed, the status of professional expertise will rise in most areas of activity, partly because of the privacy issue and also because the wealth of information will require professional interpretation. The problem of privacy is just one of the emotive issues for the community which, with other social issues, will need to be carefully understood and explored at all ages.

If the community is dependent for its success on the added value of the talents and skills of the individuals that make it up, there is a need to ensure that they are developed and encouraged. The community could operate on the industrial system of deciding that it needs a certain number of welders, librarians and doctors and expecting them to appear in exactly the right quantities, but in the information society it is the variety of talents and skills that provide the added value that is needed. Out of the mixture of interests and enthusiasms will come a range that gives the community its character, but that means encouraging people to offer what they have, not necessarily what some planner dreams is needed.

There will be many changes in activity throughout an individual's life, and on each occasion there will be a need for specialised knowledge and expertise. In some activities, for example medical practice, the changing specialities will be small shifts in concentration from one area (say obstetrics) to another (say genetics), maybe in response to new interests or local needs, maybe because of improvements in technology. In other activities the shifts may be more considerable, say from information science to management, or a total restart from working as a bricklayer to maintaining the cables of the information network.

Such specialist knowledge has to come from retraining of some kind. In some cases employers may provide it but in others it will be the responsibility of the individual. Time has to be set aside for this, and in the information society changes will be expected to be supported by training, not just new on-the-job experiences. Working with an expert as an 'apprentice' may suffice, but usually it will mean a form of 'course'. The term is in quotes because the nature of the course is often likely to be different from that which is meant by the word at present. For example, the use of a college will not necessarily be the norm, and when one is used it may be purely as a tutorial consultancy rather than as a delivery centre. Practical skills may be learned at work areas which have been designed for this or they may be in a college. The variety will be considerable.

Predominantly the sources of the training will be through packages of some kind. Again, their delivery and style will be varied, ensuring that all types of approach to learning are covered and supported. For example, some will be prepared purely for self-instruction, some for mixtures with group and tutorial involvement and some for class attendance. The materials may be delivered directly from electronic stores, downloaded to the home base (perhaps via satellite) or they may come, for example, as videodiscs or booklets. The diversity will be considerable. Using them appropriately will require skills in learning, which have been carried forward from other experiences and constantly redeveloped as techniques improve. Choosing the 'course' that suits the learning styles of individuals will be important, and while help may be forthcoming from educational consultants or programs that analyse their behaviour, much will depend on appreciating their personal style and selecting that which matches it. Part of personal development is learning to understand the methods of learning that suit one best, and keeping this analysis up to date as age and experience affect and change it.

The materials and 'courses' may come from within the community, developed and supported by local people. The opposite end of the spectrum will be international courses, usually on topics with a small potential clientele (perhaps one or two in any particular community), and delivered by available international expertise. Setting these up will come from decisions made by one of the many international networks, although professionals in education and training will be essential partners.

Networks are the final topic in this review of the information society – the glue between its diverse parts. They will exist within communities; perhaps in some cases people would describe them as sub-communities. There will be job networks like a lawyers' club, interest networks like the UFO society, leisure networks like the drama group, health networks like the ramblers' association, spiritual networks like the Methodist church congregation, and so on. Operating within a community, they will meet to influence its vitality. Another set of networks will operate at a regional level, sharing expertise in various topics between communities and enriching each other. The national networks will operate in the same way, in part attempting to influence national decisions, essential for such activities as national sports leagues or highlighting national areas of research interest. Finally, there will be international networks, sometimes including sub-sets like the European Community.

The effectiveness of networks will be much enhanced by the way in which the technology improves communication, bringing speed and coverage to dialogues, discussions and conferences at international level. Through them, individuals working in their own communities will share knowledge and news of policies, materials, activities and developments. Keeping up to date in a rapidly changing world is important, whether this concerns techniques for repairing antique porcelain and china or new rules of volleyball. Where there are only a few people in a particular community interested in a specific topic, national and international networks are places in which to test approaches and attitudes, check one's methods of dealing with problems against those of others, and identify areas of new opportunity for development. In a society that is threaded by the concept of collaboration, the use of networks to foster this is essential and communities will hold people's membership of them in high regard.

Networks should be seen as facilitatory, not dictatorial, bringing together views, information and people, providing professional advice to influence decisions, and supplying a mechanism for the generosity of sharing expertise. Run by professionals for professionals, messages from the networks will carry authority and conviction but their status is advisory and not mandatory. They work alongside governments and industry – not in place of them. Understanding the value of networks is important for everybody, and feeling able to participate in them, at whatever level, is part of an individual's contribution to the community and to society.

Conclusion

Those then are the main parameters of the information society, both in broad physical terms and in the identification of some of the needs of the people living in it. In no sense should these descriptions be considered more than frameworks and directions. Whether one likes the description or not, these are the inevitable trends of the results of the technology. It may not be a society in which one feels comfortable, although there are many aspects which I find attractive. There will be many social problems but I have not attempted to identify them, even if it is not difficult to surmise what they will be. Such a description would be speculative and uncertain, whereas the rest almost wholly is going to occur. Economic difficulties such as investment in cabling can be raised, but they are as much part of the transitional problems of today as are the inadequacies of present software to provide the range of facilities that are needed. In looking at the future it is easy to see today's issues and difficulties as perpetual inhibitors of progress, when in the broad timescale of generations they are temporary hiccups that may not even make their mark in history.

Many details are not included. Some are omitted because they are uncertain, but most are missing because they do not affect the thinking about the curriculum. Those that are included are there to help in interpreting the picture being drawn. It has not been the intention to give a complete description but sufficient to ask questions about the curriculum. Change to the information society is not performed by the cutting of a tape at a certain hour on a particular day but a gradual evolution and development. Arrival is clear only historically, not at the time. It is therefore difficult to forecast when it will be fully in place, but those entering school today will find most changes will be there soon after they leave.

It is for that reason that a reconsideration of the curriculum is needed now, not then. It is not difficult to see that today's curriculum has little to offer that will help children to prepare for the information society. Dominated by academia and having little relationship with industrial, commercial and social activities, it has been widely criticised as irrelevant and unhelpful. New thinking is needed now if children who will be at school in the next decade are to develop the skills and attitudes needed for the information society that they will meet when they leave. Education is not an instant process, and that is the trouble. Pouring boiling water over the brain grains does not produce an instant skullful of knowledge although, to listen to some of the critics of education, that is what they expect. Time, experience and consideration are needed to help individuals to own their knowledge and wisdom, and preparation for that has to begin now if they are to be ready for the future.

In the next chapter, an attempt is made to describe the parameters of this curriculum. It is derived from the basis of the information society sketched out in the sections above, for it is to live in that society that today's schoolchildren are being prepared. This is the larger impact of the technology on the curriculum, that on the whole ethos of the educational provision. As we move into a time when the curriculum is laid down by parliament, or rather by the Department of Education and Science, it is important that the approach is relevant and appropriate. To what extent does the DES view match what follows?

For some people it may not seem to matter whether we carry on with the same old curriculum or move into the new, but the prizes of the future, influence over decisions and the power of communities, and industrial and commercial prosperity, are awarded to those who are ready first. The country, more especially the communities, with children and adults trained for the information society will flourish in it. Having the right curriculum does matter!

References

Barron, I (1979) and Curnow, R *The Future with Microelectronics* Francis Pinter, London

Bell, D (1973) *The Coming of Post-Industrial Society* Basic Books, New York. *Also* The social framework of the information society, in Forester, T (Ed) (1980) *The Microelectronics Revolution* Basil Blackwell, Oxford

Bolton, E (1987) The debate on a national agreement on the curriculum and its implications for standards. In *NUT Education Review* Vol 1 No 1. Spring 1987

Burkitt, A and Williams, E (1980) *The Silicon Civilisation* W H Allen, London

Evans, C (1979) *The Mighty Micro* Victor Gollancz, London

Jenkins, J and Sherman, B (1970) *The Collapse of Work* Eyre Methuen, London

Large, P (1980) *The Micro Revolution* Fontana Paperback, Glasgow

Martin, J (1978) *The Wired Society* Prentice Hall, New Jersey

Nora, S and Minc, A (1980) *The Computerisation of Society* MIT Press, Cambridge Massachusetts (English translation)

NEDO (1987) *IT Futures … IT Can Work* HMSO, London

Stonier, T (1983) *The Wealth of Information* Thames Methuen, London

Toffler, A (1980) *The Third Wave* William Collins, Glasgow

Vallee, J (1984) *The Network Revolution* Penguin, London

Chapter 6

The Parameters of a New Curriculum

Introduction

To paraphrase Eric Bolton's aims of education quoted in the last chapter, they are to stimulate the development of personal abilities and to prepare an individual to participate in society. In any discussion on the curriculum, it is as well to have these constantly at the back of one's mind.

This chapter is concerned with the curriculum for the information society, but that has to be considered in the context of broad discussions on the subject that have been taking place, in particular over the last 12 years. These have concentrated as much on developing a framework in which the details can be inscribed as on the content itself. There have been many contributions to this discussion, started by the Ruskin speech and followed by critiques from industry, the Department of Education and Science, politicians and academics. Various additional comments from HMI, committees and councils have also been made. Strangely, none that I have read has considered the impact of the future information society, most of the contributions reflecting the issues of today in the light of general educational thinking. Perhaps many of those writers have forgotten that a curriculum started by a child now ends two years into the next century when society will be very different.

The trouble with the word 'curriculum' is that it needs translating. For Stenhouse the school curriculum was a combination of the planned intentions of the teaching staff and the actual experiences of the child. The so-called 'hidden curriculum' was part of the whole. One consequence of this definition is that it incorporates the teaching approach and learning methods as well as the content. Commonly, as here, content and methods are separated, the reason in this case being that the impact of the technology on methods deserves a chapter to itself rather than just being confused with issues of subject matter. However, it is important to recognise them as one whole issue, each having a significant effect on the other and the totality forming the curriculum itself.

Perhaps the most thorough of recent definitions of the curriculum is by HMI:

A school's curriculum consists of all those activities designed or encouraged within its organisational framework to promote the intellectual, personal, social and physical development of its pupils. It includes not only the formal programme of lessons, but also the 'informal' programme of so-called extracurricular activities as well as all those features which produce the school's 'ethos', such as the quality of relationships, the concern for equality of opportunity, the values exemplified in the way the school sets about its task and the way in which it is organised and managed. Teaching and learning styles strongly influence the curriculum and in practice they cannot be separated from it. (HMI, 1985)

So the curriculum is that which goes on in school – both the planned and the unplanned bits. Many of the discussions have centred around the framework and attitudes to deciding the content. The debate has oscillated, but there is much more consensus from the professional educators than is sometimes credited. In 1981, the Schools Council published *The Practical Curriculum*. Six ways in which schools could help their pupils were listed. These can be summarised as acquiring knowledge, skills and practical abilities; developing qualities of mind, body, spirit, feeling and imagination; acquiring understanding of social, economic and political order; appreciating human achievements in art and science; preparing for adult life including work, leisure and social participation. The sixth one was particularly highlighted:

To develop a sense of self-respect, the capacity to live as independent self-motivated adults, and the ability to function as contributing members of co-operative groups. (Schools Council, 1981)

There is an undercurrent of similarity between this description of the framework and the list of six purposes of learning that appears in the White Paper *Better Schools* (DES, 1985). This list starts with the need for lively, enquiring minds with the ability to question and argue rationally; and application to tasks. It continues with the need to appreciate human achievements; to use language and numbers effectively; to acquire understanding, knowledge and skills for adult life and understand the world in which they live; and to develop personal moral values, respect for religious values and tolerance.

One of the groups that has been promoting a new approach to the curriculum has been the Education for Capability movement, sponsored by the Royal Society of Arts. Its manifesto, while acknowledging that the need to acquire and use knowledge is important, lays particular emphasis on creative skills and 'the competence to undertake and complete tasks and the ability to cope with everyday life: and also doing all these things in co-operation with others'.

In the promotional documents for Education 2000, a project based around the six secondary schools of Letchworth Garden City and designed to move education there into the age of information technology, there is a declaration that the project is seeking changes in schools. These, the statement says,

... will better develop in young people knowledge of a broad span of human experience to enable them to show an informed awareness of possible alternative futures; skills of dexterity, analysis, invention, problem solving, communication, and decision to help them to be effective in their working and personal lives; attitudes of co-operation, responsibility, optimism, enterprise and courage leading to their self-confident participation both in the creation of resources and in community development at all levels from the local to the global; a sense of values encompassing truth, justice, freedom, beauty and compassion to enable them to make their own judgements about the uses of knowledge, skill and wealth. (Education 2000, 1985)

The project is also very keen to see the whole community of the new town involved and participating in the educational activities. There are distinct overlaps between these views and those contained in the statement of needs enunciated by the Association of British Chambers of Commerce in their leaflet *Business and the School Curriculum*. This suggests that employers are looking for the following qualities in children when they leave school:

> the ability to learn; the ability to get on with other people; the ability to communicate; reliability; basic literacy and numeracy; and an understanding of how the community's wealth is created.

Eric Lord, in a very thorough analysis of the development of views about the curriculum, notes four perspectives which reflect the different attitudes that have emerged over recent years. He states them as:

1. Views about the nature of those ways of knowing through which human beings understand and interpret the world, and of what constitutes intrinsically worthwhile knowledge.
2. A view of the culture which children are inheriting, an inheritance into which education helps them to enter and to evaluate, with the curriculum seen as a selection of elements from that.
3. Perceptions of the present and prospective character of the society and the global community of which children are part, and judgements about the knowledge, skills and competences they require as they come to contribute to society as citizen, worker, parent.
4. What are held to be the intrinsic needs of children, whose growth as persons the curriculum they experience promotes in ways appropriate to their individual characteristics and attributes. (Lord, 1988)

Lord suggests that these different perspectives have been satisfied in the statements of the White Paper, *Better Schools* (DES, 1985). It also seems likely that they are four parts of a whole. Each has something to offer to the design of the curriculum, one more important than the others in particular topics. While it is certainly possible to see conflict between them, it is equally possible to see them side by side within the total activity of a school. An examination of any of the descriptions of needs that have been given earlier sees each of these four perspectives reflected. The argument will therefore be on the weighting given to each.

Turning now to the area and elements of learning that HMI produced, they suggest nine areas, specifically stating that none applies to a single subject but to all. The areas are 'aesthetic and creative; human and social; linguistic and literary; mathematical; moral; physical; scientific; spiritual; technological' (HMI, 1985), and the elements of learning are knowledge, concepts, skills and attitudes. Three of those are clear, but it is worth listing the headings for the groups of skills: communication, observation, study, problem solving, physical and practical, creative and imaginative, numerical, personal and social. The overlaps between the two lists are obvious, but none the worse for that. However, relating them to the four perspectives that Lord provides shows that all are being addressed to some degree in the HMI description. The difficulty will be on achieving a reasonable balance between them in the practical implementation of the curriculum.

The other feature of the discussion has been general agreement on the principles which should be reflected in the curriculum. First enunciated by Sir Keith Joseph at the North of England Conference in Sheffield in 1984 and repeated in *Better Schools*, they are breadth, balance, relevance and differentiation. HMI in their document added progression and continuity. While there will be much debate on how each is shown in individual subjects, it is not difficult to see most of them taken into account. The tendentious one is balance, interpreted in the White Paper as 'each area of the curriculum should be allotted sufficient time to make its specific contribution, but not so much that it squeezes out other areas' (DES, 1985) and this is the same, only longer, in the HMI booklet. What each 'area' is can be argued at length, and the separation between them is increasingly difficult to determine. One person's balance is certainly another person's bias.

It is notable that the many voices that have been raised in discussions leading to the views expressed above have not been in strong opposition. Some have seen the march of technology and, to some extent, science as a threat to the survival of the humanities, but few have argued fervently against the general tenor of these views. Where points have been made, they have tended towards arguing about the weighting and emphasis of the various ideas rather than diametric opposition. Against this considerable background of documents and discussion, the national curriculum has been launched. Surprisingly, it received a complete round of disparagement by professional educators. Naturally some supported the proposals, but these have proved to be very few in number. If the background views against which it was prepared were so widely accepted, it is strange that so few of them appeared to permeate the writing of the national curriculum document.

The time for official comment was limited, but the *Times Educational Supplement* (1987) has provided a forum for many contributions. Extracts from some of these illustrate the range of concerns that have been expressed.

Michael Duffy, head of King Edward VI School, Morpeth writes: 'Shorn of its subtext of norms, targets and testing, Mr Baker's framework looks extraordinarily like the model that most schools follow now'. He continues: 'To HMIs "elements of learning", for instance, it comes no nearer than the vague assertion of certain "themes" that "can be taught through the foundation subjects" … You don't help schools to think by turning them into production-line machines, delivering a pre-packed curriculum to statutory quality control.'

For Chris Davis, head of Queniborough Primary School, Leicestershire, 'Real education is about self-confidence, self-esteem and practically useful skills and abilities. It is not about learning how to jump through certain specified hoops on four set dates during a school career.'

'It may not be education, but it will certainly be efficient' is the view of John Mann, Director of Education, Harrow. But 'does this model of the curriculum correspond to what we want to know about the growth of young children and how they come to understand their world? Why is there no mention of careers, economics, morals, politics, the environment and many other themes relevant to adult life and work?'

Missing, claims Peter Cornall, Senior County Inspector, Cornwall, is 'all that makes for the well-being of people, their relationships, of their homes and families.'

Certain beliefs are fundamental, suggests Bob Moon, head of Peers School, Oxford, 'that ability is a concept embracing the full range of talents, not just performance on the continuum provided by the grammar school curriculum;… that the content of learning cannot be divorced from the process of learning and that assessment must be integral to teaching and learning if it is to have any meaning; … that the historical divisions of knowledge bear no relation to the applications of knowledge, today or in the future.'

This last point is taken up by Maurice Holt, St Mark and St John College of Higher Education, Plymouth: 'The curriculum pupils are to have prescribed for them puts the clock back to the last century. Subjects reign supreme … The entire document is steeped in the mechanistic assumption that schools can be run like biscuit factories. Providing the skills and technology are there, backed by clear objectives and precise assessment, the right product will roll off the assembly line.'

Professor Dennis Lawton, Director of the Institute of Education, London University, continues the theme: 'I have two specific complaints. First, the draft is entirely subject-based in its thinking. Second, important areas of human experience such as politics and economics are almost completely neglected … To have a discussion on a national curriculum based on a list of subjects (with time allocations stipulated) is to take the curriculum debate back at least 20 years.'

To conclude this sequence of comments, here is an extract from a piece by Mark Hewlett, head of Quorn Rawlins Community College, Leicestershire: 'The national curriculum's aims [are] to give pupils knowledge, understanding, skills and attitudes to equip them for the responsibilities and challenges of adult life and tomorrow's world ... It isn't good enough to fall back on to a somewhat arbitrary list of subjects without specific reference to these aims. The disconnection between aims and curricular plans seems to be the endemic disease of curricular planning in this country and unless amended, the national curriculum will show that in the late 20th century the policy makers still couldn't get out of the ruts of traditional thinking that has dogged education throughout the century'.

Much of the criticism that has been laid at the door of the current curriculum has stemmed from some comments from industrialists who are short of people with particular skills. The cry was for more children being trained in the appropriate way, although there has been a dearth of information about what that should be. Yet, when pressed, the comments from industry are much less specific. One example from commerce is quoted above, the abilities required from school leavers being very general. In 1986, Sheffield University undertook a survey of industrial views of specific vocational training at school and found that the majority opinion was for broad and general education. Specific techniques in information technology were not required.

This view of a broad curriculum was repeated at the OECD meeting in Paris in March 1988. Akio Morita, Chairman of the Sony Corporation, is quoted as making 'a plea for greater emphasis on general education and less concentration on specific technical skills', and the Australian education and training minister, John Dawkins, is quoted as saying that 'the social sciences and humanities were necessary to help people adjust to the pressures imposed by social and economic change'. (TES, 1988) It is also clear that vocational training in school is not supported by the National Economic Development Office. Their report, *IT Futures ... IT Can Work* (NEDO 1987) advocates education in school that targets on general skills such as problem solving and learning how to learn rather than specific IT techniques, and it too criticises subject separation and the academic elitism that pervades the current curriculum, particularly in the later years of secondary education. This may be concerned only with information technology, but the conclusions are drawn as if they reflect a much wider view from industry.

Eric Lord (1988), reflecting on all the discussions and debates on the curriculum, sees a more eclectic approach arising in the thoughts and practices of those concerned with laying down its principles and shape, unfortunately at odds with the national curriculum document.

> This eclecticism is manifest in a number of ways, not least in a broader description of the curriculum and the purposes it serves. If there ever was a time when the curriculum could be described in terms of a list of subjects (and it is doubtful if it ever was simply that in the reality of the work of teachers), that time has passed. ... An understanding of the curriculum which includes

areas of learning and experience, essential elements of learning, and intentions which involve important implicit learning (for instance those to do with pupils' personal and social development), requires that insights from many quarters are laid under tribute, rather than taking any one to be the single or dominant source of truth.

Moving away from the rigidity imposed by subjects provides the opportunity to approach learning with a greater freedom, to find links between knowledge that has been separated by artificial barriers up to now. It may then be possible to achieve what Mary Warnock (1988) is looking for, a curriculum to 'equip [the] student with transferable skills and transferable expertise'.

This brief review of the discussions of the last decade has been given to provide a context within which it is possible to examine the needs of the information society. The survey in the last chapter suggested that at least the following aspects, picked out as keywords, could be identified as essential prerequisites for life in that society: flexibility and adaptability; self-confidence and co-operation; spiritual and philosophical insight; an entrepreneurial attitude; curiosity and imagination; technological understanding; practical and creative skills; using information; communication; collaboration, moral and social values; participation; cultural appreciation; and health activities. Add to those knowledge, skills such as problem solving and activities to encourage the development of personal abilities, and the picture is similar to those definitions drawn by HMI in their areas and elements of learning, or to the other documents mentioned. The interpretation by teachers in order to be relevant to their society may be different, but the broad descriptions of curriculum purpose are not incongruent. In the rest of this chapter, some suggestions for putting together a viable curriculum are presented, again in broad terms rather than specific details which would require much more space.

Domains of study

In the information society, the broad aims of education that were quoted from Eric Bolton stand. They are almost timeless in their applicability. The principal aims of the curriculum proposed below amplify those broad statements in a way that gives more guidance for their practical application. They are deliberately developed from those used in the White Paper, *Better Schools*.

1. To help pupils to develop and maintain lively, enquiring and imaginative minds and the ability to question and argue rationally from a basis of information, and to apply themselves creatively to the completion of tasks.
2. To help pupils to acquire understanding, knowledge and skills relevant to

adult life, their community and the flexibility for employment in a fast-changing world, and to communicate their views in a variety of ways.
3. To help pupils to use language and numbers effectively.
4. To help pupils to develop personal and moral values, respect for religious values, and tolerance of other races, religions and ways of life.
5. To help pupils to understand themselves, the world in which they live, the interdependence of individuals, groups and nations, and to develop the self-confidence to participate and co-operate with others in contributing towards the prosperity of that world.
6. To help pupils to appreciate human achievements and aspirations, and to develop their own creative, practical and physical abilities.

The areas of learning and experience listed by HMI are also relevant to the curriculum for the information society. To help to produce a complete picture they are quoted here again: aesthetic and creative; human and social; linguistic and literary; mathematical; moral; physical; scientific; spiritual; technological. They were chosen as attributes that should permeate all the activities of the curriculum, although they do, of course, dominate the work of certain aspects. To them, three more should be added: curiosity; self-knowledge; value judgement. The need to foster, sustain and encourage curiosity in every part of learning and personal development is essential, if pupils are to extract the information and understanding that is available to them and continue with a positive attitude in adult life. From this approach, they will have the motivation to develop interests, to seek new opportunities and to participate in the cultural development of society. Self-knowledge is particularly important with regard to learning how to study in and out of school, but it will also help pupils and adults to be more sensitive to their motives and behaviour. This is not an encouragement to psychoanalysis, but self-understanding at a more superficial level. It continually asks the question 'Why?' and creates a sense of personal insight. Value judgement is needed to ensure that the status and worth of everything is constantly considered. This may apply to the quality of information, the practicality of design, the beauty of sculpture, the elegance of a mathematical solution, the rhythm of a poem or the sincerity of a conversation. Passive acceptance of a view or even its instant rejection is socially dangerous as well as disingenuous, and pupils need to develop personal criteria for reaching value judgements in every type of field.

HMI also produced four elements of learning – knowledge, concepts, skills and attitudes. To the list of skills, it is appropriate to add decision making, and in the range of attitudes being sought, mostly social in the amplification given by HMI, that of entrepreneurialism needs to be included. In the flexible atmosphere of the information society, this is an important attribute to be developed.

In the introduction to this chapter, four principles running through the design of the curriculum were listed: breadth, balance, relevance and differentiation. HMI added progression and continuity. With the exception of balance, all are appropriate and valuable points of analysis for development of the organisation and content of the curriculum for the information society. Balance is omitted because in a flexible workplan which accepts the reality of the impossibility of maintaining divisions between pieces of study, any calculation of proportions of time is inherently fudged and contrived. In any year for any pupil, the proportion of time spent on one study domain will differ from that at other times and for other people. Learning is not an experience that can or should be locked to specific time-spans, at any age, but should fit the needs and capabilities of the pupil or adult involved. Any attempt to ascribe percentages of time or hours for the completion of particular topics infers the belief that the human brain is equivalent to liquid chocolate waiting to be processed into bars. Regrettably for those ruled by stop watches, it is not.

The suggestion here is that for the information society, the curriculum is divided into five principle domains of study, for convenience called *literacy, numeracy, technology, information* and *communication*. In describing them below there will be inevitable references to traditional subject names, but these are included for ease of reference and description rather than because they need to persist in the future. Each domain should be studied through themes, not just in the primary school but in later years as well. Such themes should be chosen and developed to explore topics that are relevant. In establishing them, particular note should be taken of the participation of local industry and commerce in developing knowledge and understanding of its different aspects. Each pupil does not study each theme in the same way. Instead, the programme of work is developed individually for each child and determined with them, not just imposed. On many occasions, the agreement may be to work as part of a team with other pupils, where each is aware of the contribution he or she is expected to make. Thus, the system remains flexible but also monitored to ensure progression.

By introducing the concept of domains of study, only two of which have close connections to traditional subjects of the curriculum, it could be assumed that an attempt will be made to demonstrate that there are strong, hard divisions between them. Nothing is further from the truth, for it must be patent from the beginning that they overlap continuously. Although in learning the mind asserts patterns and separations in order to be able to cope and deal with the world, creating false ones for children that are not applied later (except in some academic circles) seems peculiarly nonsensical. Instead, the domain divisions are selected for their functionality. Each is dominated by different skills and attitudes, but even here there will be overlaps between them. It is hoped that pupils will not leave school believing there are divisions, but that instead, in most tasks, there are elements of each.

All children will tackle all the domains of study throughout their time in compulsory education. Those with lesser ability in some topics will pursue them to less depth than those with more. Some topics may be omitted if they cannot be achieved, but bright pupils will explore concepts and knowledge further as prompted by their interest and ability. To do this, the topics will be arranged in modules which may be taken to different depths. Modules will not necessarily be linked to particular domains of study, although this will be the normal arrangement, but may be taken at any time under the guidance of a teacher. This does not mean that as soon as a topic is found to be difficult the child stops doing it, for pursuing understanding through difficulties is one of the disciplines of education. On the other hand, if in the teacher's judgement the pupil has reached as far as ability permits, then it is appropriate to move on to a different piece of work.

In the descriptions of each of the domains of study that follow, no attempt has been made to provide the full content or even specify all the aims. This would take far more space than is available here. Instead, broad descriptions of the scope of each domain are given to indicate the range of possibilities within it. Without the availability and use of the new technologies, a curriculum designed in this way and with the amount of flexibility and self-determination that is envisaged would not be possible. Both in the ability of the teachers to manage and monitor the progress and development of each individual pupil, and in the potential variety of ways in which children can approach and tackle each topic, the power and options that are necessary have been made possible by the technology. Just as life in the communities within the information society will promote the importance of the individual, so the curriculum as expressed through the domains of study will appear directed specifically to the needs of individual pupils.

For parents, the standards of achievement of their children will be seen in the degree of success they have within the range of modules pursued. No module will be 'better' than another, but tackled at different stages of progress not necessarily linked to age. Different abilities and areas of interest will emerge as important to some children and not to others, but this will not signify one as being superior to another. The acceptability of concepts like this, like the whole idea of domains of study, is difficult to appreciate at a time of transition when the ethos of the information society is not a clear part of the general ideology.

Literacy
A great deal of authoritative writing has already been produced about language, including the Bullock (1975) and Kingman (1988) reports, and much too from the National Association for the Teaching of English. Planning the details should take these into account, but the comments here are restricted to showing the scope and attitudes that would be important in this domain.

Literacy is concerned with interpretation and communication. While the latter is considerably expanded in the domain of that name, it is essential that much communication through language and various media is undertaken in this domain as well. However, literacy is concerned with interpreting the meaning of messages, in whatever form they appear. Primarily this refers to verbal messages, both written and spoken, but it is also necessary to consider body language, graphics and pictures, extending them into symbols. All these also are a form of language which requires interpretation and are essential elements of the literacy of life. The symbols of weather forecast charts, of national flags, or of the standards carried by Roman legions, bear important messages to those who see them. Acknowledging their meaning is part of this domain.

However, reading, writing and speaking will form the dominant part of the study. In writing, wordprocessors will play a significant role but there will continue to be a need for handwriting as well. As the study continues, much attention will be paid to the structure of the different forms of language. Drama, film and television, as much as written and spoken elements, should be part of this study. Books and the cultural tradition of national and international literature will be essential parts of the work being undertaken, but radio, film and television scripts should also be introduced in the studies. The technology is a considerable aid in using this material, and programs that support textual analysis of books will give extra insights into the way in which language can be used effectively.

Pupils will be encouraged to examine the different structures of language as it is used in written and oral forms. There are contrasts and similarities to be explored which encourage interpretation in each case. Poetry too should be examined for its particular quality of expression. Rearranging its patterns, accompanying it with music, changing odd words, all easily done with the technology, affect the interpretation of the message, and children should explore the effect of this. Such explorations are part of the study of the structure of language.

Role-play exercises are another means of using language, identifying issues of disagreement and methods by which they are resolved. Many conflicts arise through misunderstandings derived from the misuse of language. Failure to communicate meaning is overcome by the good use of language, and that involves the employment of appropriate structures. Individuals develop personal patterns of language which each can identify, and which change over time and under the influence of such various factors as the current fads of street credibility. Recognising this is part of the understanding of language development.

Themes could be developed around the various ways in which language is used. For example, language is used to give instruction, and a great variety of examples are available – technical manuals, timetables, routes in stately homes and introductions to examinations being just a few. Reports, whether administrative or journalistic, are another use of language, and studies can include videotex, propaganda and advertising, television, and radio commentary. Jokes too use language and, depending on the form of presentation, use it in different ways. The joke on television is different from the same one on a printed page if each is to be effective.

Studies in this domain are likely to use games with words and graphics to explore meaning and interpretation, for using language is fun, and playing with words and meanings is part of entertainment. The game 'Consequences' was and still is a great success because words stimulate enjoyment and pleasure through their manipulation and incongruities. Nonagrams and Dingbats are currently similar sources of entertainment, and word derivation can be turned into similar enjoyment. This could lead to children taking extension studies of classical languages, for example, because the concept of derivation becomes exciting and interesting to them. These are all activities that the technology can stimulate within the broad study being done in this domain.

Dialect and language development, including that of graphics and other message carriers, will help to relate the study to the community and its occupations. All this should involve practical activities, including writing, discussion and argument, drawing and the preparation of materials that can be used within the environment. Underlying this work is the preoccupation with interpretation and devising criteria of personal judgement.

Numeracy
This domain of study is clearly linked to mathematics, about which a great deal has also been written. The outstanding document is the Cockcroft report, which would be taken into account in any detailed planning. The following comments are therefore intended only to demonstrate the scope and attitude of this domain.

Numeracy is about quantification – the 'literacy' of number but with the purpose of using number to interpret the world and to solve problems. In the comments that follow, the utilitarian approach has been overemphasised, but that is because it is so often understated.

The structure of number is an essential basis from which to develop numeracy, but it comes more sensibly from the use of calculation to solve problems and to investigate issues than from a regimen of learning rules. That does not mean that mental flexibility with numbers is not an advantage, but not all individuals develop that easily although they still have to attain a level of numeracy. Most people can derive pleasure from playing with numbers or symbols, for the patterns and relationships that occur are entertaining, extraordinary and intriguing. Representations can be very pleasing aesthetically, as well as providing insights into the mechanisms of the physical laws under which we live. From such games and explorations, structures, functions and rules can be derived, together with strategies for logical analysis and problem solving.

The technology has provided instruments that are considerable aids to probing the patterns and relationships of number. Simple programming, databases, games, simulations and graph plotters are just a few of the computer techniques that are available, and there are other useful devices as well. One of the advantages of these instruments is that they take much of the tedium from calculation, where the work on that is not essential for the child's learning. Concentration is on the concepts, not the chore of calculation although, on most occasions, the pupil should be able to estimate an approximation of the answer so that the one which appears is known to be of the right order.

One aspect of numeracy is the interpretation of numerical data, whether presented as a collection of figures or symbols or as a graph. This is particularly important with probability and statistics which are so widely used to make cases for decision making and action. Thus this domain is concerned also with interpretation and communication, for it is as important to be able to use numerical data to present a case of one's own as it is to interpret the other person's.

Themes of work in the domain will gain a great deal from being related to the concerns of the community and industry. Part of numeracy is being able to read a balance sheet, whether of a company or a country. This includes understanding, for example, the influence of inflation on employment and the trade balance, and recognising the difference between figures that describe quantity and the feelings of individuals that describe quality. I have done a great many calculations about apples in baskets with my children, but we never discussed how many were bad! Figures are presented with an authority, the degree of which needs to be understood.

Domestic balance sheets should also be included in this domain. These may be about, for example, household budgeting, food intake and its nutritional value, or spatial design. Study of this may lead to modules on textiles which have only a small amount of numeracy in them but which are perfectly acceptable as part of the extension of an individual pupil's interest.

Another exploration within this study could be a graphical/numerical representation of the flow of water from rain through a river to the sea. A wide range of extensions of study are possible with such a theme for those who would gain from pursuing them, but in itself the representation shows other uses of number. Other topics could include ecological relationships in an environment based on the statistics of the different populations; Pert and Gantt charting and the development of costing exercises; or the numerical evidence used for decisions on the building of roads. The possibilities are endless for everything that involves the use of quantification and number can be developed as a topic in helping children to progress in their numeracy.

Missing from this list is the option that some will take, which is the development of the sheer pleasure of number through further exploration of relationships and rules. While for some pupils the utilitarian side of numeracy and extensions from that is appropriate for their development, others will find additional satisfaction, skill and knowledge acquisition from taking the abstractions of mathematics further. The domain has room for both – the excitement, enthusiasm and interest of individual pupils being the key factor.

Technology
This domain is not just Craft, Design and Technology (CDT), as it is now taught, although there are close affinities. It incorporates, for example, some of the topics taught in science, geography and home economics, so it is broader in scope and its extension studies can go further afield.

Three main principles guide the selection of themes in the domain: preparation for life in the technological world; the three-dimensional developments of man to control and exploit the environment; and the impact of technological progress on society.

In preparing for a life which is to be dependent on technology, it is important that pupils develop an understanding of the concepts and principles behind the devices and mechanisms being used, which may be those needed to monitor the environment – such as those measuring temperature, humidity and pressure for agricultural planning – or pieces of technology such as electricity generating turbines. The approach is technological, not scientific, so the theory of electricity is unnecessary whereas the structure of a motor is important. Extension studies could include that theory, the chemistry of corrosion, coefficients of expansion and so on. Not only will pupils be expected to understand the concepts, but they will also develop appropriate practical skills – for example cutting a screw or soldering a resistor. Time will be spent on considering the issues of safety built into mechanisms and structures as well as environments.

Emphasis within the study will be on the way the technology solves particular needs. A theme might look at the disposal of sewage, examining its constituents, how it is transported, the natural and artificial methods used for breakdown, the disposal of different parts, and the dissipation of destructive elements through dilution. Such a theme would incorporate substantial elements of all three sciences, some geography and home economics, but the system is essentially a technological mechanism for solving a particular human need.

For the second principle, the study would emphasise the development of projects to solve problems. 'Design and make' would be the underlying spirit of the work, although not every problem would be taken through the 'make' stage. The study would pay particular attention to design, for one of the strange truths of technological development is that an efficient technical solution usually results from an aesthetically pleasing design. The quality is therefore important, and the study could examine houses and glass fibre cables as well as examples of natural design such as plants and animals, rocks and rivers. Such an analysis would examine why the designs are successful in the conditions in which they operate, and would help pupils to identify the reasons behind effective structures.

Materials too need to be examined. Properties need to be understood to identify the differences between them and to what they contribute. Finally mechanisms that man has used to control and develop the environment come under scrutiny, from levers to motors, from pneumatics to electronics. It is the concepts behind the mechanisms that are important in order to achieve the appropriate insights but, as in all this work, extension studies into the relevant science should be available.

From this background, children will undertake projects to solve real problems. The community, industry and commerce would be involved in supporting this work, so that it is done against a perspective of interest within the adult population. Costing analysis needs to be included to add a sense of reality to the exercises. The pupils would normally work in teams, and effective collaboration would be encouraged.

Many of the central studies examining the way in which man has used technology should be done by everybody. Earlier in this book, I quoted the old adage that Latin was a good training for the mind, and it seems to me that the modern equivalent is probably basic electronics, the kind of exercises that are done at present with the 'Microelectronics for All' kit. This is a three-dimensional exploration developing problem analysis, strategies of thinking, planning and forecasting, logic and simple manipulation, some numerical skills and an insight into scientific experimentation. There are other educational benefits, but this is enough to suggest that for modern life it is an appropriate array for mental development, equivalent to that produced by that old language for a time when we were tied solely to the verbal attributes of education.

Undertaking study in this domain will benefit from a wide range of programs and other uses of the technology. For example, simulations of experiments and structures will be invaluable as will computer-aided design and make systems. Without the benefit of such learning materials, the work would be difficult to organise and lack a sense of reality.

The third principle examines the impact of technological development on society. From the people in the community will come attitudes that can be developed by pupils through discussions and arguments. Religious principles would be introduced and developed within the debate, as would an appreciation of the decision-making structures of society – locally, nationally and internationally. Thus, the domain would consider social and personal reactions as part of its examination of the way in which mankind seeks to control and use the environment. For some, the practical elements of the study will establish an empathy and interest which may influence their decisions on their personal future, while for others it will be the planning and theoretical aspects that will catch their interest. However, all pupils will undertake a mixture of both in their study, although there will be a range of extension studies to expand and develop interests in any particular area.

Information
Much of education for children is spent on the acquisition of knowledge about the world and how it works, and the great majority of that is based on existing information. The information domain is concerned with the collection of information and turning it into knowledge. The process is basically similar throughout, although different emphases and approaches may be needed at times depending on the topic being examined. However, the fundamental activity is finding relevant data and information, analysing it and turning it into knowledge and understanding.

The world is determined by the natural laws that govern it and the human impositions that have shaped it. It is the interaction between these that has produced the state in which we currently live, and will continue to amend and alter it in the future. The natural laws and conditions as well as human impositions and the rationale behind them have to be understood, for only through knowing about them, and their interrelationship and the influence each has on the other, can individuals find the context in which they can affect the future. The vitality of society is dependent on an appreciation of that interaction and the choices that people make in relation to it.

To amplify this a little, and therefore to show the scope of the domain, here are a few examples of the kinds of interaction that are referred to above. The physical laws of gravity need to be understood if the economic cost of space travel is to be considered. Through the reactions of molecules, fertilisers are created that affect food production and the quality of water. From an understanding of the conditions of living things, the impact of a building development on the ecology of a valley can be forecast. Over millions of years, natural laws have shaped land in certain ways that make it attractive for a settlement, but its arrival accompanied by a reservoir damming a river affects that shape. Some settlements developed in areas because of the fertility of the environment, but have disappeared through changes in trading conditions and the ambitions of certain people. Others have changed through pressures created by social and physical conditions, or the effect of powerful religious beliefs.

Underlying study in this domain is the need to appreciate this interaction between natural laws and human interference. In order to do this, both have to be explored and understood independently as well as through their impact on each other. Without knowledge of photosynthesis, there is no rationale for arable farming and the value of cabbage in the diet. There is a great deal of existing data and information which pupils can use to help them to create their knowledge.

The principles for this domain are the acquisition of knowledge of natural laws and conditions, patterns of human behaviour and the interaction between them; the development of strategies for finding data and information, using this to form views and draw conclusions; and an understanding of the factors that influence decisions and behaviour.

The collection of data can take many forms. These will include searching databases; monitoring the environment; sampling activities and polling, perhaps through questionnaires; observation; measuring, both directly and through sensors of various kinds; doing experiments, both in real time and by simulation; collating views on issues; making records and exploring other people's records. From this assembly of data it is necessary to provide a structure to turn it into information. This can then be manipulated, cross-referenced and processed creatively into knowledge that can then be used. Thus a wide variety of techniques and skills will be developed and employed in approaching the studies in this domain.

Themes that can be used to link the studies are numerous. They might, for example, include energy, life forms, forces, origins of the community, patterns of local life, and cultural and spiritual influences on the shape of the environment. Determining a range of these that will promote a good basis of knowledge is crucial to success in the domain, and they also provide openings for extension studies into particular subjects that excite and interest the pupils.

Gathering the data and information from various sources is only the first step. There is then the need to assess its validity and accuracy, measurements from scientific experiments probably requiring criteria different from evidence obtained from war-time despatches. However, the value of the work with information is in the way in which the views and conclusions are presented. Essays or report-writing are not the only means, although they have their place, but a range of presentation methods should be encouraged.

Another principle involves appreciating the factors that influence decisions and behaviour. Behind this is the need for pupils to understand how authority and attitudes are managed and developed so that they can influence them later for themselves. If a tax is altered, how can they comment effectively? If a factory continues to discharge waste into the air, how can it be influenced? If children continue to demand chips, where is the evidence to change their minds? What is required is an appreciation of power structures and economics, as well as factors like social conditions, disease and deprivation. Nor is the study here confined to the community or national interests alone; it should also be opened up to the influences brought by and within other countries.

The study provides the opportunity for a wide range of extension studies, developing particular areas and questions that have provoked interest. While much of the work in the domain is concerned with developing knowledge, approach to the study will involve active learning and a range of projects and assignments. Whatever the topics or themes chosen, the underlying consideration is the influence of human activity on natural laws, so that pupils can gain a perspective from which to judge decisions in the future.

Communication

While literacy was described as interpretation and communication, with the emphasis on the former, this domain is similar but with the emphaisis on the latter. Of course, this means that interpretation is an essential element of the study as well, but that pupils will be more concerned with the communication aspects. True communication is a dialogue involving, for example, listening as well as speaking, and in this study the listening part may be taking note of and responding to reactions as much as it is actually participating in a discussion.

The thread for this domain is self-expression, conveying messages. Many mechanisms are available for this, for example two-dimensional design, foreign languages, art, music, drama, dance, film and television. All are means by which ideas, views and emotions can be described and explored. Other forms of communication such as sign language, sema-phore and morse could be introduced, although at a minor level for this is not a study of communication as a theoretical notion but a practical and creative use of different mechanisms.

The principles for the domain are the ability to listen, read, observe and interpret messages in forms other than English; use foreign languages and other forms of self-expression to communicate; and develop personal criteria for judging creative achievements.

The domain is therefore concerned with the expression of ideas and emotions and the exposition of conflicts, tensions and conversations. While this may involve the creation of a piece of music or a dramatic dance, it also envisages discussions with people from overseas about mutual interests. All are forms of communication, and the ability to use them, or at least appreciate their value, is a necessary part of education. Some may find the mechanics of painting or playing an instrument are beyond their skills, but electronic forms of this can be used by everyone; indeed, much modern music is played with electronic instruments. Two-dimensional design can also be achieved electronically if the physical skills required when using paper or card are inhibiting; in fact, this is often the more appropriate way of doing it. Visual essays would be a form of communication that would be expected from work in this domain.

Much of the study would take place in groups and teams as in the other domains, but solo efforts would be encouraged in some forms of communication. Painting, sculpture and solo instrument work are obvious, but there is also solo dancing, some acting, personal writing and so on. Part of the teachers' intent will be to identify natural or acquired ability, so that extension studies for its further development can be encouraged. For the pupils, part of the purpose of the study is to find methods which suit an individual as a means of expression and emotional release. Viewing these forms of communication as methods of undoing internal tensions is as valid a way of approaching them as using them as powerful ways of presenting a particular case.

Knowledge of foreign languages is needed to conduct conversations around the world. Visits and sharing studies and projects with pupils in other countries are methods of showing how valuable the knowledge of other languages can be. Comparing the way of life of communities in this country with those overseas stimulates interest and creates a broader perspective of the world. Thus, this part of the study should be approached in a practical and purposeful manner so that, at the least, children will have the confidence to conduct a general conversation in a foreign language. For more detailed study of the language structure and literature of other countries, extension material would normally be used.

This attitude of practicality and purposefulness should be behind much of the study in this domain. While the personal release approach is perfectly justified, there should also be an endeavour to create with a message of meaning in view. Such a message may be the realisation of a scene or a musical description of a mood, but children should be able to express the intent of their communication. Working through such creative activities illuminates a much wider range of knowledge and experience than is seen in the act of communication itself.

By surrounding pupils in atmospheres created by other people's communication, it is possible to help them to determine their own criteria of judgement of quality. There is no right answer, and as age and atmospheres change so do the values placed on particular items. However, it is never too early to begin the exercise of pursuing the establishment of personal judgements and attempting to express them. But underlying this, as with all the study in this domain, is the process of self-expression and conveying messages.

Health

This is not a domain of study, for most of the knowledge linked to it will be touched on, if not explored, in the other domains. However, in the information society, time will need to be given to the presentation and discussion of contemporary issues regarding health. Personal health decisions become more important with affluence and the strange mixture of foods and other indulgences that people will seek. Today, looking after one's body includes being aware of issues such as drugs, smoking, AIDS and, probably, food additives and there will be similar issues in the information society.

The most important part of the time given to health will be concerned with exercise. For some years exercise will be an essential element of a pupil's time, giving benefit from both individual and team activities. Later, however, such exercise will take place as part of and among the rest of the community. Part of the time will therefore be spent examining and sampling the alternatives available and choosing those which are both suitable and interesting. Thereafter, participation will be expected, but alongside and with the rest of the community. There are likely to be continuing school teams and school events, in competition with other communities and countries it is hoped, but participation in these will merge with similar activities within the community.

While there will be no compulsion, the expectation of the community will be that people will participate in activities they have chosen because there will be a conscious concern with maintaining health which, without exercise of some form, will gradually fail. In order to sustain encouragement, a great variety of opportunities will be available from which to select. These will also be offered at a range of levels and expertise so that all will feel able to join in without any sense of personal shame or inadequacy.

Specialisation

This curriculum is designed to promote a broad education for all children. Dropping subjects early and therefore having to make decisions about a pupil's future before there has been time to mature and reveal natural abilities will be avoided. Concentration on particular aspects will come and go as the interest of the pupil and the guidance of the teachers waxes and wanes. Specialisation at an early age locks the child in a straitjacket of progress along certain predetermined lines, similar to the life-style of the industrial society, whereas in the information society choices and interests are constantly changing with the flexibility that is part of the way of life, and this is reflected in the way the curriculum is kept as fluid as possible. There will be core areas of learning in each domain of study, but these are the concepts that all pupils need and can manage, and which provide the links to extension studies.

Thus the workplan within each domain of study is planned with much free space for taking and developing these extension studies. Their selection will be guided by the interest of the pupil and the advice of the teacher, and they may be undertaken singly or in groups. There is no pressure from a choice of career or even from further education, although the close involvement of the community in the work of education will inevitably influence the content of some of the extension studies.

Some of these will be academic, developing theoretical knowledge, while others will be more practical in intent. Each extension study will be a module of variable length with a number of break points for children of different abilities. Levels of detail will be selectable so that quicker children with more interest can probe a topic further, while the slower pupils may only achieve a general understanding of a broad concept. By taking a particular selection of extension studies, a pupil may develop a deep knowledge of, for example, life in Roman times, and this could be conceived as a piece of specialisation. However, the treatment will normally be broad rather than locked solely to historical evidence in order to reflect its relevance to the present day. Studying the Romans just because they are interesting in themselves will be the kind of activity that takes place outside the basic education of children in these early years, and would be shared at that time with many others with similar interests.

Guiding children in their selection of extension studies will be a key role for teachers, and will place a considerable burden and responsibility upon them. It is the nature of the professional role of teachers to act as consultants on learning, which is another way of looking at this part of the work. A good set of courses will unlock a flood of areas of interest from children which they are eager to develop, and helping them to select the most appropriate with the provision of adequate time is going to be a difficult task. The aims of education and the principles behind the curriculum and the various domains will act as guidelines, but in the end it will be the teacher's understanding of the pupil which governs the advice that is given.

Work within the extension studies would continue to support the elimination of traditional subject divisions that should be evident in the description of the domains of study. For example, pupils wishing to develop their understanding of the external respiration of man could find themselves needing to learn about the chemical constituents of air, air pressure and such influences upon it as height above sea level, and also pollution and the issues affecting it. Bright and enthusiastic pupils may pursue this by examining the influence of partial pressures of individual gases on oxygen diffusion and the Bohr shift, but this is hardly relevant for the majority who merely wish to understand in broad terms what is happening.

For some children, the extension studies will involve doing more of the same work they have been doing - art, some craft work, reading more literature for literacy are simple examples. An extension study may be the most appropriate means of providing the opportunity to study a topic by doing more of it and thus improving skills or developing deeper knowledge. Other pupils may find themselves doing studies that involve them in closer work within the community or local industries. These would be assisting with the study domains in any case, but in these extension studies there would be additional involvement. For example, study of the influence of religion on different communities may include visiting and working in a variety of centres of worship over an extended period of time.

The extension studies are not related to particular careers or job lines, although being a good conversationalist, for example, is a considerable asset for someone who will be working in a shop. One principle behind them is to help children to keep away from ruts, and from being stuck in one area of interest at the expense of others or of narrowing their options. The target is variety, so that study remains an adventure into the unknown as well as the practice and establishment of a range of skills and insights.

Tackling one's education in this way requires flexibility, for new aspects are constantly emerging and the repetition of exercises is kept to a minimum. Confidence too is generated, because the learning techniques that pupils develop help them to study in every domain – a good preparation for the uncertain future.

Preparation for many outcomes

In the information society there is no certainty about the future pattern of continuing paid activity. Change is endemic and perpetual. Pupils moving from the time of compulsory education face a way of life in which there are potentially many different possibilities, several of which may be explored by a particular individual. Any future direction chosen at this time is therefore subject to change and must be looked at from this point of view.

The types of activity have been noted earlier, and can be derived from an examination of the description of the information society given in the last chapter. In this section, I want to identify some of the different ways in which further training and education will be offered. These will encompass all types of paid and unpaid activity, and there is no hard separation between them.

The purpose of the curriculum has been a broad education and the establishment of general skills, not the training for a particular career or job. Hence, after completing this education specific training for particular jobs or interests begins. For some, the amount of training may be minimal: so many of the 'chore' activities require only an identification of the area of work and the position of the tools to do it. For others, the amount can vary between weeks and years, depending on the level of knowledge and skill necessary to do the work.

Within the community, there will be close liaison with the various schools so that pupils are aware of the openings for work and may even have established early links with employers. Organisations and industries will provide any special training required, directly or through colleges or other methods. Some people will join national organisations which will also provide appropriate training for the work required. Of course, young people may arrange for their own training in the hope that they will then be more attractive to organisations or companies, but this would not be the normal situation with a workforce of some size. However, such an initiative may be their best way of approaching garden-shed industries or starting their own business.

For children going on to higher education, different patterns may exist. Substantial changes in oganisation and attitude may be needed to achieve this, but for the information society the following may be the most useful. Some students will enter higher education with sponsorship from an employer who feels that a particular specialised degree course would be valuable for the work required. The sponsorship would be tied to a job with that organisation for a certain period of time.

Those entering higher education without sponsorship would take less specialised degrees than those frequently (though not always) on offer at present. Each would have options that encouraged particular interests, but the outcome of the course would be a broad degree through which a student had developed skills, attitudes and knowledge to a higher level than before. For some organisations and industries this may be more attractive than the specialised courses, as it would provide a continuation of general education. On receiving a job, many of these students would need to continue at higher education doing a postgraduate diploma that provided the specialisation needed for their new future. Normally this would be sponsored, but a community may pay for it if the small employer or garden-shed industry could not afford this. Such courses would also be taken by people doing retraining to upgrade their knowledge and skills.

This need for constant retraining is necessary not only for those with higher education backgrounds; all adults will need the opportunity to retrain in order to develop new interests, change the direction of their work or update themselves. A wide variety of retraining options will be available in addition to higher education, and the following list is only a sample of the different types.

Some opportunities would be provided by colleges or similar institutions, and in some cases by in-house facilities within an organisation or industry. These would usually be course options, together with good practical facilities to support them.

Another option would be through open learning schemes. Tutorial support may be on offer to accompany them, but they may also be taken without it. The materials may come through a variety of means, television and via satellite from other countries for example, but this would be in an organised scheme.

A further option will be private study. This means that there is no organisation behind the scheme, but there will be many opportunities for the learner to link up with members of the community to share the study or to receive advice. One of the information facilities of the community will be the names of people who are willing to offer their help with such private study. This will be used particularly for DIY training and the development of personal interests.

Dividing the options up like this suggests that each is separate from the other. However, this is not true for there will be many combinations of approaches – for example a piece of private study developing from ideas generated on a course at a college. Just as every other aspect of the society is flexible, so are the opportunities for retraining and learning new tricks and trades.

Conclusion

Unlike the description of the information society itself, there is no sense of certainty that a curriculum like the one above will be forthcoming. There are many vested interests in maintaining the current rigidities and divisions. The changes in higher education hinted at in the last section will be the source of much discomfort and unwillingness.

The present curriculum has to discard the traditions of separate subjects, which for many have become totems of security and reassurance at a time when that is hard to find. Each of the subjects is now overcrowded with 'essential' material – good for the bright maybe, but is it always so important for the average and less able? Anything new can be added only if something else is removed. Such battles and scrambles cannot continue, if we are really concerned with the needs of the individual child. Outdated material is kept in syllabuses, sometimes with admirable intentions, sometimes with feeble excuses about keeping the context or 'they may meet it when they leave school'. Regrettably, sometimes it is retained because the school cannot afford to replace equipment with modern versions. If it has to be used, it finds a place in the curriculum!

The information society is different, and it does need a different preparation. The curriculum proposed here does meet the principles outlined at the beginning of this chapter and supports the needs of people entering that society. With compulsory education based on such a curriculum, children would progress into society more able to adjust to its effervescent changes and uncertainties. However, to adopt it does mean starting to design again, and after the many changes in education in schools in the last few years that is not easy to do. All that can be said is that it is such a different arrangement that it would be very enjoyable doing it. At the end, teachers would know that they had developed the groundwork for the education of individuals who were going to make the information society a prosperous place, not sending out more of the same for a production line that has long since closed down.

If the communities in this country are to prosper within the world at large, then we need to be prepared early for the information society, and our children trained to benefit from it from the beginning. On the international scene the preparations are being made already, not yet planning in the form outlined above but getting much closer to it. At a conference at the International School of Geneva in February 1988, educators there began to put together views for a curriculum which has many of the features described here. There is an urgency in getting the shape of the curriculum ready for the future if people are to be prepared for the society that follows and to take advantage of it.

But Stenhouse said that a curriculum is both the plan of what one hopes to do and what one actually does. The latter can be interpreted partly as how children study and learn the curriculum and that is what we turn to the next chapter. Without the facilities provided by the technologies, the curriculum described above could not be implemented and managed. It will be no surprise that these same technologies will also play a significant role in helping the pupils to learn.

References

Bullock Report (1975) *A Language for Life* HMSO

Department of Education and Science (1985) *Better Schools* HMSO, London

HMI (1985) *The Curriculum from 5 to 16. Curriculum Matters* 2. HMSO, London

Kingman (1988) *Report of the Committee of Enquiry into the Teaching of the English Language* HMSO

Lord, E (1988) The whole curriculum, in O'Connor, M (Ed) *Curriculum at the Crossroads* Schools Curriculum Development Council, London

NEDO (1987) *IT Futures ... IT Can Work* HMSO, London

Schools Council (1981) *The Practical Curriculum* Methuen, London

TES (1987) *Times Educational Supplement* 18.9.87

TES (1988) *Times Educational Supplement* 1.4.88

Warnock, M (1988) *A Common Policy for Education* Oxford University Press, Oxford.

Chapter 7

Learning in the Future

Introduction

The best designed curriculum is successful only if children are taught appropriately and learn effectively. This chapter is concerned with these issues, for if the new curriculum is to be adopted some changes in roles and attitudes will need to take place. Like all such changes they will be disturbing to the confidence and security of teachers, who will require comprehensive retraining and development work, but these are normal problems in the information society. Some people may even find that the approach and attitudes needed do not fit their own perceptions, and the education system may therefore not be the best place for them to continue to work. Adjusting to that is part of the consequences of the new age into which we are moving.

The new curriculum requires approaches that offer greater flexibility, leading to a greater degree of autonomy for the pupils. It is important that as they grow older they have increasing control over what and how they learn, for that is the situation of the society into which they are moving. As adults, they will be choosing the courses and studies that they feel are needed to develop their interests or retrain their skills and knowledge, so that the attitudes they developed as children should have prepared them for making the appropriate decisions and discovering how to go on from there.

Because the approach to learning is designed to be adventurous and stimulating to their curiosity, children will need to have greater freedom with the resources that are available to support their studies. It is not helpful to be too restrictive in allowing access to items that can be used. Developing a sense of responsibility for the needs of other people and working with them is part of the background to society, and care for the resources of others is part of this. The target is self-discipline not the discipline that comes from stern external supervision.

Relationships between children and teachers will also be changing. Continuing respect and acceptance of some authority will still be necessary, but the role of teachers will move from being the source of education towards that of educational consultant. The implications of this will be discussed later in the chapter.

Also affected by this curriculum will be the role of the school. When the technology first appeared on the scene in education, there were some people who suggested that schools would disappear as all learning could take place at home. While theoretically this is true, it suggests an image of school education that is restricted to the kind of industrial curriculum that we have today. The learning experiences necessary for the information society require places where collaboration can be fostered, consultancy can be given and a sense of community responsibility can be developed. Whether the environment is called a 'school' or any other name is not important, but there is certainly a need for a place where such learning can occur. To appreciate the necessity for this, consider first the approaches to learning that are going to be used.

Approaches to learning

Learning does not occur in a vacuum. A child does not learn without a background of experiences and even some knowledge. From the earliest years learning has been taking place, often with no assistance. Much of what is learned may not be considered academic but it includes, for example, talking, a sense of direction, and a feel for differences in materials – all of considerable value later. Learning at school is designed to build on that experience and to involve the knowledge that has been gained outside studies that take place within the curriculum. Frequently, though, credit is not given for the learning that children have gained outside the school environment, just as insufficient credit is given to adults on courses for the knowledge and skills that life's experiences have given them. Through the influence of the Learning from Experience Trust a change is taking place in adult education, and it is to be hoped that the same spirit comes into the schools. If much is to be gained from the new curriculum, the contribution of experiences from outside school have to be recognised.

Processes and outcomes

The watchword for much contemporary interest in learning is experiential. By working with materials or being involved in exploratory activities, the quality of learning is enhanced. This goes together with support for the processes of learning as being of significance in the development of the pupil. Undertaking a project which involves the categorising of information helps the child to understand that procedure and develop the relevant skills and techniques. All this is admirable; by using various strategies and methodologies the pupil will understand them more, but usually in the context in which they were used. The difficulty with concentrating on processes is that they take place within the learning activity and therefore are not necessarily noticed. Without recognition, it is most unlikely that they will be transferred to other situations in a different context, and there are many examples of teachers reflecting on how this has failed to occur. The lessons of a mathematics topic are not used in solving a similar problem in physics. The construction of sentences, fully understood in an English class, are not used in a history essay.

Experiences are immensely valuable and need to be built upon, just like the learning experiences that have been absorbed from activities outside the classroom, but this only occurs if the generality is drawn out and exposed for the pupils to understand. Leaving it within the learning of a topic ensures that it is locked to that context and is not used elsewhere. It is also lost if there is no sense of success in the topic in which it has been used. Because the process of learning is rightly seen as most important as it produces the array of skills, strategies and techniques that children need, there has been some neglect of outcomes. Pupils do not study a topic for the pleasure of the process, although that can be attractive, but to achieve a goal. During a piece of work there may be a series of outcomes, of course, each one providing knowledge that is used in developing the next, but it is necesary for children to be conscious of their continuous achievement. It develops confidence, and the success enhances their motivation.

Learning needs direction and purpose, and this comes from recognising the outcomes that are being sought. There is no need for some of the absurd detail that accompanied early examples of programmed learning. 'Use that piece of software and you will find out more about how the Vikings lived in Yorkshire' is sufficient for a young child to know why a piece of material is being used and that it may also be interesting. 'Doing this piece of Latin will improve your mind' may be an outcome but is hardly likely to capture the attention. As pupils use the variety of materials prepared for the new curriculum they need to know why they are exploring them, just as much as the teachers will be aware of the range of processes they will be employing, the elements of which the children need to appreciate afterwards if they are to transfer them to other topics. Both processes and outcomes are needed together.

Learning to learn
Learning is a complex activity which still requires a great deal of research if it is to be understood. Much has been done by educational psychologists and others to elucidate the most appropriate contexts and orientation which promote successful learning, and there are descriptions of different types of learner, the most popular being the holist/ serialist division. Missing, though, is any clarity of insight into the actual process of absorbing information and transforming it into knowledge.

Courses on 'learning to learn', strongly advocated by many writers such as Irving (1985), are usually designed to help pupils to understand how to handle information, take notes, write essays, and organise the arrangements and setting for learning. Important as that is (and essential if any effective learning is to take place), it still does not get near to the process of learning itself. Other writers give guidance on memorising facts, using tricks and mnemonics, but these are decreasing in importance at a time when the emphasis is on conceptualisation.

In his influential book, *Freedom to Learn*, Carl Rogers (1969) criticises the traditional didactic approach to teaching as preventing students from developing their own ideas and pursuing their own interests. A supporter of process rather than facts, he asserts the considerable value of learning how to learn, but in doing so recognises the individuality of each person. There is no one way to learn anything; each pupil will approach it in different combinations of ways. Gibbs (1981) suggests that it is important for students to develop their own methods, perhaps even discarding the systematic arrangements for managing their learning that others had been advocating. Idiosyncrasy is valuable, and matches the flexibility and recognition of individual variability that runs through most work on learning, but a background of ordered management provides a pattern and security that many students find helpful.

These last comments bring us back to the earlier position – the organisation for learning. There is still a need to get closer to what is happening in the mind. Quite rightly, motivation is signalled as important, preparing the right attitude to learn. A good review of the different categories of motivation is given by Entwistle (1981). Being interested in the topic is an important prerequisite but is still not the complete answer. We are left with hints and clues about activities that pupils use: asking questions of themselves; using the knowledge and repeating it; breaking it up into different parts; relating it to other factors, forming patterns, creating a context; playing with the knowledge, manipulating it in different ways; making it attractive.

More important still is the chance to reflect and allow the mind to adjust to the concept or idea, and fix it in relation to others. This is part of the value of concept mapping, and other forms of rehearsal of knowledge, but it is the provision of time to rearrange the memory that seems to be the important characteristic.

Courses to help children to think are not common. De Bono has initiated some in South America with reported success, and currently there is much hope for courses in Somerset based on the work of Sternberg and Feuerstein. Their purpose is not just in supporting mental skills, but also in helping children to identify the processes that are taking place. While the learning procedure may be unique to individuals, it is helpful for them to appreciate what is useful for them, partly to develop confidence and partly to be able to select materials and approaches that they will find successful in the future. Procedures that are appropriate may change over time, and indeed may be different for different needs, but the ability to be conscious of this and identify it later is the crucial factor. By helping children to develop this self-awareness, teachers are creating a background of self-knowledge that will prove invaluable at times when retraining is necessary.

The standard techniques associated with learning are valuable and should form part of any support that teachers give to pupils. Working against a good background of timing and personal organisation will usually pay dividends in learning, but it is appreciation of the personal tricks and approaches that helps children to identify the techniques, systems and materials they are going to find of most value in the future. Part of the process is being conscious of what is to be achieved, of what the teacher wants. Much time has to be spent in negotiating targets with teachers, in working through to the essence of a problem or a topic that is to be explored. After practice, many pupils are able to do more of this analysis themselves as they grow older, but for others it may always remain difficult. Again, different personalities respond in different ways, some aiming at more precision than others. For some, the broad challenge of 'the effect of Cromwell on the structure of society' is more stimulating than an analysis that breaks this down to questions relating to parliament, royalty and the Church. Helping children to appreciate their position on the holist/serialist spectrum is part of the teacher's role in developing their self-knowledge.

This emphasis on the processes of learning is more important at a time when so much will be dependent on the use of materials. If a range that takes account of the great variety of approaches is not available, failure faces many children who could succeed in other circumstances. If people who prepare materials are not conscious that learners need such a range they are not supporting the diversity of approaches that exists. If children are not more aware of the approaches that they find most successful for themselves they will not know which ones to choose. Just as living in the information society demands skills with handling information, so learning and retraining requires an appreciation of how this is done effectively for oneself.

Participation
In approaching the curriculum, it is the position and needs of the learner that must dominate all considerations. Sometimes teachers will work through presentations as they have done traditionally, but this will no longer be as dominant as in the past. Economic as it may be, learners find it unhelpful for much of their needs. Not only is it ineffective in supporting successful learning, but also it does not help children to prepare for the circumstances in which they will be learning after they have left school. Through a dynamic range of experiences, children will

be better able to choose those which are more acceptable to their personalities and be confident in using them later. Without that exploratory study of different approaches and types of material, they will not be able to select those which stimulate and help them to understand and learn.

There are circumstances in which children benefit from presentations, from being taught directly. For example, a fast resumé of a topic or review of what is known is often provided usefully in this way. A presentation can put forward the context in which a topic will be studied, the background circumstances against which events in the past took place. Lectures are useful in providing instruction on how to undertake a survey or perform a scientific experiment. Teachers may find them helpful too in asserting their expertise and personal qualities, which can assist with discipline and relationships with pupils. Perhaps, most valuably, presentations can be the source of motivation, excitement and stimulation. A child's approach to the study of a topic presented with dynamism and conviction can be transformed from reluctance to enthusiasm. Extension studies can be selected because the topic has a relevance and interest that would not have been apparent without the introduction such a presentation inspired. Part of the role of teachers is to sell enthusiasm for the topics they are encouraging the children to learn, and such salesmanship can come from good presentations.

Beyond these circumstances, however, the part played by class presentations is limited. The majority of learning comes from pupils' active participation in their learning experiences, not passive reception or even tedious note-making. Nevertheless, children need a personal record of their activities – something to use to revise their knowledge – and the approach to study needs to encourage this. Active participation, though, means that the emphasis is on exploration and finding out rather than being told, and thus on exercises that require all pupils, in different ways, to be involved in activities rather than merely receiving.

Some of these exercises will need to be organised. Skill and technique development, for example in art, craftwork, scientific experiments or using a turtle, will need some organisation although the amount will differ in each case. Some research tasks will be prepared to ensure that the appropriate skills are developed for use later in more open circumstances. Sometimes exercises in mental agility are valuable in sharpening thinking and enhancing confidence, and these too need management. For younger children group activities will be arranged, so that in later years they can be organised by the pupils themselves. Much time will be spent in school on group discussions and debates, leading to presentations to other pupils and even seminars. After exploring topics, groups will describe their conclusions to others, probably involving them in activities as well, and the preparation of such presentations will form a significant element of different studies.

For some of this organisation, teachers will be presenting core themes to different groups in order to give context and a sense of direction to the open studies that will follow. For example, field work and attachments in the community and industry will need preparation, even though the activities themselves may have a freedom to explore and experiment that may lead to diversions. The balance between opening up opportunities for expanding interests and ensuring progress and personal development within a reasonable timespan requires sensitivity and deft handling as well as insight into the ways in which children study. Achieving this satisfactorily is part of the professional acumen of good teachers.

Self-direction

The major approach to learning will be directed by the children themselves. Given problems and tasks, guided by their personal interests and aided by the wisdom of the teachers, children will pursue their own learning activities. Most of this will take place in teams working together on issues but, as necessary, individuals will study alone, perhaps with the object of contributing an aspect to the deliberations of a team. This approach will be based around the concept of supported self-study, opened, extended and where necessary amended to be applicable to children of all ages.

To be successful, the scheme needs tutorial support – that is, the guidance of professional teachers who are not necessarily expert in subjects that children are studying at a particular time. The level of intervention of these teachers will be much higher with young children than with older ones. The target will be to reduce intervention to a minimum, but young children will need more guidance and support in helping them to develop their confidence and general maturity. However, the emphasis will be on the rapid achievement of self-direction. For younger children the teachers, acting as tutors, are likely to have all the expertise that is necessary to resolve problems and difficulties, but older children will raise questions and areas of interest that are beyond their knowledge. Such questions should not be left unanswered as far as is practicable. Part of the tutorial role is guiding the pupils to sources of information, other techniques of approaching the issue, and different methods of finding out. However, if this fails access must be given to expertise that may be available within the school, on offer from local advisers or lecturers in higher education, or obtainable from the experience of people living within the community. One of the benefits of the closer relationship between the local community and educational provision should be closer liaison between the knowledge and skills of people and the needs of those who are learning. This will be important when they become adults, so children need to expect and relate to similar experienced support when they are at school. The wisdom and knowledge of the community is its strength and the source of its vitality, and this must be as available to those learning in the education system as to those outside it.

Thus the tutor may not have the expertise, but can help children to uncover the various possibilities by which it can be found, even to the extent of using the experience within the community. Another role is monitoring the work children are doing - advising on its value, giving guidance on its direction and suggesting links to other activities. A balance children have to find is the management of their time between topics and within the exploration of a particular interest. Firmer guidance will be given to younger children than to those who are older and who should have acquired certain personal skills and understanding so they can deal with the balance of time themselves. Being successful with the techniques of a titration can be so satisfying that a pupil may wish to continue with repeated experiments or computer simulations for a considerable time. No more is really learned, but the fuel of personal satisfaction keeps the activity going much longer than is of educational value. Is it to be stopped or is this satisfaction important in generating a reserve of confidence that will be useful in the pupil's personal development? Making that judgement and preparing the appropriate advice is the teacher's responsibility.

Another issue with time is knowing when to limit the struggle for understanding. The pursuit of a particular interest may lead to a quest for knowledge that is beyond the capability of the child. Understanding population pyramids may be attainable, but comprehending the social and religious pressures on Bengalis that create a particular one may be too demanding. Identifying these limits and being satisfied with a more superficial level of understanding is difficult for the pupil, when it seems that only a little more time need to be spent to master the whole. Good tutoring takes note of the problem and provides appropriate advice.

Resource management
Without good management and organisation, and the support of an information service that provides rapid data about the facilities inside and outside the school, none of this is possible for a large number of children. It is attainable through judicious and planned use of databases and profiling programs using the new technology. Tutors need immediate access through terminals to the information bank of the school and to the community, national and international databases. As appropriate, pupils also need similar access, although there will be some confidential areas from which they will be barred. The organisation and management is not a complex task as long as the needs are analysed carefully. Ease of use is paramount, for the tutors must not spend a great deal of time learning the mechanics of accessing the information.

Additional programs would help tutors and children with the selection of materials for study, probably derived from an expert system. Essential to this would be an analysis of the learning approach that was appropriate for an individual pupil using both deduced information and the child's own self-knowledge. Such analyses would become part of the pupil's profile for future reference and perhaps amendment. The information from the system would provide guidance on progression as well as the selection of materials, but the emphasis is on the word 'guidance'. The tutor, the person with expert knowledge or the pupil may each decide to ignore the guidance for all manner of reasons relating to their particular perceptions of the present situation.

The materials available for study will be wide-ranging in content, approach and format. Some materials need not be substantial but just a plan for practical work. Others may be a mixture of guides, books and programs for study over several weeks. Some may lead to lengthy study, while others may be completed in an hour or so. It is the diversity that is important, not just in the information that is supplied but also in the range of learning approaches that can be used by pupils in exploring them. This means apparent redundancy of materials, for some will be used rarely as only a few children may wish to pursue a certain topic in that particular way. Excluding that item would deprive those children of their opportunity to learn, reduce the variety of experience and insight available within a community and introduce unnecessary deprivation. Breadth and variety in the collection of resources and learning materials is thus essential in order to support study of a high standard for all children.

The materials should also foster a range of experiences, as it is at this time of children's personal development that they should be sampled. Such experiences should span both the practical and the theoretical, inside and outside the school environment, and make use of a diversity of formats. Undoubtedly, computer-mediated items will play a dominant role, incorporating a range of appropriate adjuncts similar to the videodiscs and controlled manufacturing instruments of today. The present use of simulations is the forerunner of systems of exploration that should form a significant proportion of the programs. They are designed to foster curiosity and stimulate further questions. Using the technique of switching in different parameters, the depth of study can be adjusted to match the ability of the pupil. Study packages would contain the program which would be used in the general operating environment that was familiar to the pupil, rather than in its own, so that ease of use would be increased by the absence of any anxieties about how the software behaved. Additional material could be gathered from remote databases by on- or off-line links and, of course, pupils would have further support by searching databases and using communications facilities. The study packages should not be conceived as complete in themselves, but as stimulants to adventures down a variety of paths and byways as the interest and problems develop.

At the end are records of achievement, presentations and reports to others, and the sharing of experiences. This may be within a team where one member has pursued a topic to contribute to a project being developed by the whole group. It may be to a whole class or merely to a teacher, but the aim would be to share the knowledge gained, particularly in an extension study. Perhaps a package is created in the process which could be added to the collection of resources that are available. Just as the study packages include a range of formats, so should the display of outcomes. For example, visual essays through the software control of a selection of pictures would be one form, videotex displays with graphics another, a working model under computer control a third. There are many more.

Keeping the packages up to date would be one requirement of the school organisation. Liaison with industry should ensure that the latest knowledge and techniques are incorporated where these are relevant. Some study materials may be downloaded from local, national or international collections for processing through the school's own desk-top publishing and similar arrangements to be added to the collection. Again, good management with the assistance of appropriate programs should ensure that warnings and checks about the quality and the contemporaneousness of the material were received and noted.

Thus, the principal approach to learning would be conducted through the pupils' own selection of directions for study. Their techniques would be mutually identified and, as closely as possible, matched to those in the various study packages. While the range of topics would be broad, the monitoring and profiling would ensure that progression and coherence between the studies were maintained for individual children. Various keywords would dominate the planning and activity: curiosity, autonomy, interest, confidence, self-knowledge, judgement, participation, co-operation, creative learning, exploration. Ensuring that these are kept at the forefront of each child's development and study is yet another function of the teacher.

Teachers and pupils

In considering the role of teachers in this new curriculum in the information society, it will be clear that the changes are not as extensive as may be thought, certainly for those who have been steering the classes they teach towards resource-based learning. Most of the attributes that will be necessary have been within the common practice of many teachers for several years, and the appearance of the GCSE has stimulated others. However, for parents looking back to their schooldays, the roles will seem very different, the emphases on pupils' individual needs appearing to be very strange to those who were at school in the 1950s and 1960s. For the good teacher of today it will not seem to be such a change, for the same skills and approaches are needed, just the weighting on each being different.

Familiarity with the technology will be presumed and expected. All teachers will not be programmers, though many will write their own materials within fifth- and sixth-generation frameworks. Some, who will be the experts in their schools in this area, will have experience and considerable knowledge about the technology. Ease of use for the majority will come from the familiarity and clarity of purpose of the interface between the equipment and the teacher. Because they will be using only a few of the different forms of interface, all the programs they meet being imported into that environment, there will be no discomfort or anxiety. All will be familiar.

The most significant difference is that the role of giving out, of telling children about the excitement of one's special subject, will be much reduced. True, there will be occasions when it will be the appropriate thing to do, but the old class teaching role will be much less important than being the reference point as the specialist in a subject, preparing learning materials especially for extension studies and talking to individuals or groups about the more interesting features as they provoke attention. Not every teacher in a school will have an area of expertise to demonstrate. All, however, will have the role of educational consultant, acting as guide and mentor to the pupils as they go about their learning. Some of the features of this role are outlined below, divided rather artificially into sub-groups for no role is ever separated in practice in this way.

Supporting pupils' personal development

A number of the activities that are associated with supporting the personal development of children have been described earlier, sometimes at length. There is the need to help them to think and learn, and to recognise as far as they can the techniques and styles that suit them personally. This is part of their growing awareness and self-knowledge, a significant aspect which needs to be recognised and understood.

One aspect of learning to learn is self-organisation. Not only is it valuable for private study at home, but it also helps considerably in preparing for and reaping benefit from the use of study packages. Children need the guidance of teachers to develop personal strategies and methods to arrange their activities in a planned and managed manner. This is likely to include how they handle their personal information stores which will be dominated by computer-related devices.

Successful learning is the object of all these activities. All pupils can achieve to some degree, and identifying the processes they go through in doing this is important in creating self-confidence. However, it is also valuable to identify the strategies and methods used in reaching success in particular topics. For example, most people in education accept the need for problem-solving skills, but understanding the personal procedures that are involved is a critical stage in being able to apply them. There may be alternative methods in different situations, and so it is likely that individual children will have a number of such strategies that they can use. These are not taught, but emerge during exercises like simulations. As the guide to helping children to learn, the teacher's role is to go back over what took place as the pupils tackled the problem and help them to identify the steps that were taken. This is just one example of the processes and skills that children will be developing as they learn, and teachers will have to help them to identify many others as well. A few, like some basic mathematical procedures, will form part of the instructions for tackling a task, but the majority will be determined after an exercise is completed.

Much time will also be spent by teachers in helping children to work out their needs and interests. While on some occasions the teacher will feel it necessary to push strongly a particular direction for progress, the object of the emphasis on pupil selection is that they become increasingly responsible for their own learning pathway. A proper balance between ensuring progression and the acquisition of relevant knowledge on the one hand, and the freedom for individual choice and personal interests on the other, has to be created. Personal discussions, with the evidence of the profile of progress from the school's databank together with any information from an expert system analysis of appropriate topics and materials, will lead to an agreement between teacher and pupil on the next stages of work. Some would call this a 'contract', but that seems more legal than is likely to be the practice. However, all this arises only after the pupils have been through the procedure of recognising their needs and interests, for which help will be needed as they may not immediately be clear. For younger children the answers may be a pathway which is strongly influenced by the teacher, while older pupils may find the use of 'careers' programs of great help.

Some of the guidance that teachers will offer will be founded on evidence from monitoring the studies that the pupils are doing. While some will be exercises that lead to firm conclusions, others will be projects that are considerably more open-ended. This monitoring will ensure that there is continual understanding of the strategies each pupil is using, and the need for diversions for further learning either during or at the end of each project. Advice on the next steps is dependent on appreciating the degree of achievement on the last steps, and this forms part of the record that is attached to the pupil's profile – the evidence for future advice.

None of this is possible without the establishment of a good rapport with each pupil. Encouragement and praise for success are useful elements in forming a personal relationship that develops trust and respect, and has always been part of the skill of good teaching. Crucial to the style of work that is needed in this curriculum, though, is the stimulation of curiosity, a trait that is common in younger children but in the present curriculum disappears in the early teenage years as pupils come to think that education is pointless. The techniques for ensuring that curiosity is maintained need to be developed and established, but they are more likely to be successful within a method of working that accepts and supports the pursuit of the pupil's own interests and is not locked to a rigid set of curricular boxes.

Supporting children's study activities

Exploration is a technique that children will use in developing their knowledge, and there are substantial periods of time when it is most appropriate for them to be left to get on with it. However, teachers will be needed to guide the planning, to help pupils in identifying their strategies and techniques, and to ensure that appropriate facilities are available. Safety is one problem that will have to be covered. It is always difficult to time when intervention is needed, so that the pupil's own inspiration and drive are not inhibited and yet progress is maintained. Technical problems need to be resolved so that, for example, inability to enter a database is overcome and the information is found. Leaving a child to try to find solutions to this by exploration may be very wasteful in time and money, unless of course this is one of the objects of the exercise. One of the disadvantages of exploratory learning is that it takes time, but learning is more successfully achieved from doing, not listening to answers, and this is a cost that has to be met. Nevertheless, judicious use of intervention can reduce the time that is wasted and give guidance on more suitable pathways to achievement.

Crucial to the information society is the ability to handle and use information. There is a medley of skills and attitudes that needs to be developed, many instinctive that children need to recognise. For younger children, exercises in interpreting information from various sources may be valuable and these will continue throughout their school career. Teachers will be helping this process, observing failures and giving guidance to better strategies. Whatever the task being confronted, the methods of finding and using information are critical and teachers have a major responsibility in ensuring that pupils can do so effectively in a variety of circumstances.

Much of this information comes from study packs and resources that are accessible inside and outside the school. Teachers also have a responsibility in seeing that these are properly managed, that access is not difficult and that their use is planned and organised. With younger children the control will be tighter, as their personal planning and ability to identify useful items will need to develop; as they grow older, such control will be lessened. Again, there is a changing position on advice in selecting items, initially undertaken with considerable teacher support, later with less. This can be achieved only if children appreciate the reasons for choosing items and are able to adapt those reasons to their own use.

Making decisions like this may be assisted by the views of peers. Setting up teams or groups to work together is another aspect of the teacher's role. Such groups need monitoring to ensure that every individual is contributing and gaining. It may be necessary to move and manipulate pupils in order to ensure a continued balance. Behind the importance of group work is the need to encourage co-operation between pupils, and recognition and support for each person's contribution. Such lessons need to be pointed out if they are to be noticed and assume their rightful significance.

Sometimes the teacher will need to join in a piece of work being undertaken by a pupil, and play the role of partner in a piece of learning. One of the attributes of the technology is that manipulating data, either directly or through a simulation, can throw up strange results. A nonplussed pupil then has to analyse and relate these to his or her own previous experience and knowledge. By intervening and working alongside the pupil, the teacher, who also may not have come across these results before, can assist in determining their meaning and relevance. The teacher's contribution is experience and knowledge that the pupil will not have; the gain for pupils is hearing and seeing strategies and approaches being used that may form part of their repertoire later.

In these cases it may be valuable to have expertise in the subject being explored. For some teachers, a significant role may be the provision of topic expertise that can be called upon when necessary as well as being used directly in leading work in particular domains of study. Not all teachers will be employed with this responsibility, but several will be. All, however, will have a role as a general tutor, an education consultant. This will involve particular care for certain pupils as well as being available in any areas where study is taking place to support and encourage the work. Not being expert in everything, such tutors must be able to provide access to help elsewhere if that is needed.

Supporting the school as an environment.

The character of the school within the community is much influenced by the teachers who work there. Their interest and enthusiasm for its various activities and for the pupils generate respect and support for it. Without that, the level of co-operation within the community will fall. Seen as education consultants, they can offer guidance and help to adults as well as to children, even if the latter are their speciality. If they are seen only as childminders the respect of the community will be that much less.

Their role in pastoral care is significant, as has been partly illustrated above. By demonstrating an understanding of the natural problems of growing and learning, by assuming relationships with pupils that show friendship as well as authority and expertise, they can assist in resolving issues and problems that are outside direct involvement with learning but which can impinge on and distort progress. This kind of support will continue to be invaluable.

The school must be seen as an important establishment within a community. As such, it needs to work with the people of that community and with commerce and industry. There must be a flow of staff between them if teachers are to remain up to date. Expertise from the community can be usefully involved in the development of study packages, and much work undertaken by the pupils may depend on activities within industry or other parts of the environment. Thus, it is necessary for teachers to ensure that relationships with the community are good and that support is strong.

These are the dominant roles of teachers in the new curriculum. Of course, the divisions between them that appear above are not real, there being many obvious overlaps. Changes from the present situation are not very dramatic, mainly involving emphasis and concentration. However, the approach to education will be different – much less direct teaching but a great deal of professional educational expertise in supporting learning. I remember that when the Nuffield science scheme was introduced, several teachers I knew rejected the 'discovery learning' approach. 'Unless I am teaching, telling the children what to do, I am not working' was the attitude many expressed. How much more difficult they will find teaching with the new curriculum in the information society.

Organising learning

In some of the futuristic writing that took place immediately after the surge of interest in the arrival of the silicon chip, there were suggestions that schools would disappear. Learning materials would arrive in the home, and using them interactively down cables or through radio transmissions, children would not need to leave for establishments like schools.

The technical capability underlining this thinking is entirely practical and much of it will be available and in use in the future. Indeed, the home and elsewhere in the community will be important areas in which learning can and will take place. But this does not mean the disappearance of schools. The arguments outlined for the curriculum and the approaches to learning suggest a continuing and valuable role for the school and for teachers as educational consultants.

From the home and environment will come an array of useful contributions to supporting learning. For example, the information network will provide valuable access to many important sources, and the expertise of the community will meet many of the children's needs. Downloading material into equipment at home will be a normal domestic phenomenon, and children will use it as much as adults. Much of their research will take place in the domestic environment; teachers will expect this to happen and not be surprised when it does. Sometimes material will be sent back to teachers via the same electronic networks instead of being presented at school, just as in any domestic interchange throughout the world. Even with such facilities, however, schools will still be necessary.

Perhaps the most obvious reason for schools is the need to develop social behaviour and interaction. Peers from within the community meet and establish relationships, often changing with age and personal development. Relationships are also established in a simulated working environment with older people – the teachers, who are neither physically related nor next door neighbours. Creating social interactions with both peers and adults are essential attributes for preparing to thrive in adult activities and participate in the community. Without the school environment in which this takes place, new arrangements would have to be made in which the same results could be generated; this would be very wasteful, especially when there is a need for schools for many other reasons.

Co-operation is a key feature of the information society, and developing the skills and attitudes for it is a necessary element of education. In schools, the emphasis on group and team work is a contribution to this; it would not emerge from the isolated individual learning from home base. Team games used to be considered as the main training ground for these co-operative attitudes, but as their importance reduces so the value of group or team projects becomes more apparent. With all the facilities that a school can provide, it is an obvious site for such work to be developed.

Indeed, these facilities are another important reason for the continuation of schools. Working with a wider range of equipment than is likely to be available in every home will provide a considerable variety of learning experiences. Laboratory equipment and access to field studies will be important too. While it is possible to download many of the learning materials into the home, the monitoring of progress and the introduction of diversity will be less effective in the absence of the teacher's advice, support and encouragement that must accompany them.

The school's own organisation has to present a much more flexible arrangement if time and access to extension studies and the development of interests are to be fostered. Some schools have considered dividing the day into structured mornings and flexible study times in the afternoon (see, for example, Rainbow 1987). Many variations are possible.

The materials and facilities depend on the presence of teachers and tutors if they are to be used effectively. If the learning is to take place with the necessary support and guidance, educational consultants need the school environment as a base from which to operate. One teacher is not enough, for learning efficiency develops from the range of skills and expertise they offer as a group.

Health activities also start from a school environment. Although many of the facilities will be used by the rest of the community, and the community's own will be used where the school does not have certain special areas, establishing the motivation for involvement and the context in which this takes place is the speciality and responsibility of the school. Without that environment, the enthusiasm of the children will be difficult to stimulate.

The process of going to school is a discipline in itself, which helps to establish a level of personal organisation that is important for the future. Coupled with the arrangements made for learning, which introduce their own organisation, pupils develop an appreciation of the importance of personal management which will be invaluable in sustaining an appropriate self-discipline in the future. As much of their activity after school will depend on personal organisation that will ensure that it is done efficiently, the introduction to its advantages through the business of being at school is helpful.

Within the community, the school will be seen as an education centre, often used by adults as well as children. It provides a focus for contacts and the establishment of relationships with the community and especially with the commerce and industry of the locality. Through the school come the links that ensure that the resources used in learning reflect the latest practices and developments where these are necessary, and where those pursuing, for example, the ecological needs of the area can meet with pupils to discuss relevant issues. In one way, the school could be described as the symbol which highlights the importance of learning within the community, not just at the level of children but throughout life. The calibre of knowledge and its continued increase are the strength of the community in the information society, and the school is an important feature in ensuring that this is recognised and encouraged.

Conclusion

Throughout this chapter, the emphasis has been on the child-centred nature of the approach to learning. The curriculum is not driven by the processing of children through a system but provides a means by which they develop the processes they need for adult life. The information society is much less of a system than that in which we currently live and much more of an environment in which there is greater opportunity for human self-expression. It is for that world that the approaches to learning are devised.

Nor is the curriculum dominated by subjects. Instead, it emphasises the variety of interests and areas of study that a child may wish to pursue and encourages that diversity. The selection of topics is responsive to the enthusiasm of the learner, although this may be stimulated by the personal excitement of the teachers. By having access to a wide variety of materials and resources, children can develop their knowledge and thinking along pathways that they find interesting. The technology is there to make access and use easy and uncomplicated, yet fast and flexible. Through a range of programs children can enter into simulations of experiences and adventure, and explore knowledge and ideas as far as their personal abilities allow. Together with the other facilities, formats of material and times of concentration can vary to suit the conditions and moods of the individual child.

None of this will succeed without the presence of teachers, acting for the most part as sources of expertise, tutors or consultants. Through their relationship with the children, progress is monitored and encouraged so that haphazard journeys are curtailed and a sense of coherence is continually achieved. There is no need for all to be doing the same thing at once, for that is rarely convenient to each child. Instead, teachers recognise the continuous adjustment of the curriculum to suit the needs of the individual, but keep in mind the broader set of principles of the curriculum which must be achieved as the guidelines behind the progress that is made. Supported by the data available through the profile record of each child, each teacher is able to monitor progress and provide guidance on where to go next. If the description of the learning organisation appears free and easy, it is the professionalism of teachers and their understanding of the pupils that give it shape.

For it is from this course of study that a child leaves school to join the adult society, which may be bigger than that of school, but with its organisation mirrored in that which went before. In the information society, individuals count as separate people within the community, just as they did at school. While they may have strings of numbers to identify them in each database, in action each is a separate person with personal needs and intentions, and that is the way they developed through school. The information society encourages people to use their personalities and follow their interests; this also is the kind of environment and atmosphere that they found in their time at school.

References

Entwistle, N G (1981) *Styles of Learning and Teaching* Wiley, Chichester

Gibbs, G (1981) *Teaching Students to Learn: a Student-Centred Approach* Open University Press, Milton Keynes

Irving, A (1985) *Study and Information Skills across the Curriculum* Heinemann, London

Rainbow, B (1987) *Making Supported Self Study Work* CET, London

Rogers, C (1969) *Freedom to Learn* Merril, Columbus, Ohio

Part 4

Progressing Towards the Future

Introduction

In the first part of this book, I reviewed a few of the developments that have led us to the present position with respect to the technology and the thinking about the curriculum. It was and could only be a selection to build a picture and context against which the rest could be written. Some people would include other events as well, for it was not planned as a complete history but merely a series of highlights in a continuing development. The story so far is not a revolution, not a series of astonishing events, not iconoclastic or cataclysmic. Instead, it is a steady progress of stages of planning, thinking and experimenting with new ideas based around the possibility of new activities brought about by new scientific and technological inventions. Sometimes these have caused changes in industry and commerce that reflect across through society to education, while at other times teachers and professional educators have adopted new devices to try to improve the effectiveness of their work.

Adopting innovations such as these is not the result of careful experiment and evaluation, important as that is. It is not the outcome of political or administrative insight, helpful as this can be in providing funds. Instead it is usually due to individuals, generally professional educators, acting with energy and enthusiasm in purely empirical and pragmatic ways. By backing them because they 'sound' right, and not necessarily because they fit a preconceived plan, colleagues and sometimes administrators have ensured that progress has been made. In the end, one can question whether it would not have taken place anyway, that the invention or the approach would not have emerged from the melting pot in its own good time, and of course there can be no way of finding out. However, one backs innovation and new ideas because they help one to jump a few rungs of the ladder of progress, getting a step or two further ahead.

The story of this set of innovations is very much linked to individuals and the provision of opportunities for them to experiment and develop. When the story stops or hesitates, fear has crept into the system, perhaps because the changes are exceeding the speed at which those who have to implement them can cope. More often than not, it is because the administrative plan is not written in a way that can absorb and adapt to the new situation. The glue of administrative planning is extraordinarily adhesive! Relying completely on professional educators also has its drawbacks, for perceptions are governed by tradition and prejudices, but on the whole the judgements are more reliable.

Once the innovation has occurred the time for evaluation follows, and that is when it should happen. However, evaluation often presupposes an agreed view of direction and purpose, matching the new with the old and measuring the value added as a result. If there is no agreement, or if the new has no 'old' with which to compare, the results fall into the bin of short-term prejudice or misunderstanding. This is the difficulty facing any innovation of a fairly dramatic nature. If the whole of the school computer investment had been dependent on the effectiveness of the first programs it would never have come about because the work was certainly done much more effectively with pencil and paper than software. Those who backed the idea had a broader vision of the capability of machines with more power and greater memory and the type of programs that would then be used.

The judgement of evaluation in this field at this time has to look at broader concepts of purpose than merely whether the topic is being learned more efficiently. It is not whether children, after using a particular program, have a clearer understanding of the origins of the First World War that counts, important as that is. Rather, it is that in finding this information they pursued certain processes that help them to understand the interchanges of decision making, have some empathy with the participants, have uncovered relevant information, and have developed some personal abilities in thinking and sorting evidence. If they do happen to know the origins at the end of the experience, it is at a level of understanding different from mere memorisation. Thus, any evaluation should be adding up these gains as well, even if they were not necessarily the aims of the program maker, the teacher or the administrator who designed the curriculum.

But even this does not present the evaluation of an innovation in its true light, because it is still focused on judgements relating to a curriculum designed, one hopes, for at least the present society. The more important judgement is whether the material, in its context, is providing the educative experience that is needed in the curriculum for a society up to 14 years hence. The judgement of the value of programs and activities in the primary school should relate to the needs of people living at that time and ask whether their school experience is providing an appropriate background. At a time when the development of society was apparently slow, it was possible, without too much error, to suggest that what was appropriate today would be acceptable in the future. This is no longer the position, for the needs in 14 years' time will undoubtedly be very different from those of today.

So what does an evaluator do? Evaluation is important, indeed essential, if curriculum design and products are to be subject to constant improvement. Even though the history of education is full of examples of good teachers making brilliantly effective use of apparently poor material, this is no reason for being unconcerned with ensuring that items are made better. One mechanism is to relate the evaluation to the design of the information society that was described in Part 3. Regrettably, many decision makers will not recognise the importance of some of the characteristics stated, and so the evaluator is thrown back to relating to the curricular purposes that have been identified by, for example, HMI. The emphasis is on the words 'curricular purposes', not whether a certain list of facts or subject concepts are learned. By describing a program or an approach with the technology through their observed characteristics rather than through a doubtful set of subject-orientated achievements, the teacher has a broader perception of their value and the gain that is possible in using them. A good decision maker can see whether or not this line of development should be supported.

For the innovator, such judgements are important and can be critical to the future. No-one should give a derogatory evaluation of a development that is slowed by the lack of the appropriate technology – if it is feasible, it will happen. Evaluating the vision is as necessary as examining the current stance. Much more important, however, is recognising the good innovator and ensuring that that person receives continuing support and reasonable freedom to develop ideas. That the progress outlined in Part 1 occurred was because certain individuals found that freedom and were given the encouragement and support to continue to create.

Where are we now?

In Part 2, I reviewed some of the uses to which the technology can and is being put in the current curriculum. These can be categorised as:

1. Providing opportunities for developing some so-called vocational skills, particularly in electronics, computer studies and business studies. These can be learned in a broad way, probably better than linked to strictly vocational ends. However, the emphasis is rightly on applications and relevance to industrial and commercial practice.
2. Improving the effectiveness of current teaching and learning. This can be through exercises and simulations relating to topics that are firmly in the centre of the subject areas, and can probably be helpful in most disciplines, ranging from stage design in drama to fortifications in history.
3. Providing new opportunities for learning that have not been available before, but which enrich and extend the current curriculum. These may

provide new ways of approaching old topics but are more likely to add to them as, for example, simulating nuclear reactions in power stations or the formation of land forms in geography.

4. Providing access to information stores and facilities for communication, allowing children to find and use data from local and international sources. This affects deeply every subject in the curriculum and encourages the promotion of international understanding in a new way.

5. Offering facilities for administrative and organisational purposes that can reduce the time teachers spend on this and increase the efficiency with which it is undertaken. This is not restricted to those teachers involved in management only; duly planned, the systems can be accessed and used by every member of staff. The value in the organisation of resources is particularly notable.

6. Providing children with the opportunity to create their own presentations in new ways. Again this affects every subject, for example graphical output of scientific experiments, painting, music, writing teletext screens or presenting visual essays with videodiscs.

All of these are exciting and stimulating ways of using this technology to enhance and improve learning in schools without the need for any curricular change. Within the present circumstances, there are clear advantages for teachers and pupils in making use of this technology to produce more interesting work and at the same time appreciate the facilities and options that come with it. However, schools are being asked to change. The national curriculum is to be implemented.

How does it fit into the national curriculum?

With its core and foundation subjects, the content of which are still under discussion, the national curriculum will focus the educational provision in schools into certain clearly stated areas of work. These will be further determined by the need for pupils to take attainment tests at certain ages which are designed to provide measures of achievement against what will amount to national norms. Information technology will continue to be of value across all subjects, just as it is now. As the approach to learning becomes more attuned towards exploration, so the advantages of simulations will be clearly identified as offering another means of working through problems. When the time for attainment tests approaches, the facility of the technology in providing revision and practice will be found to be particularly useful, as repetitive exercises and correction will reduce the need for teacher involvement.

Thus the teaching of the national curriculum will gain across all subjects from the incorporation of the technology as a stimulant for learning. Just as now, teachers will be able to continue the curriculum without any use of the technology, but the children would lose useful experiences and practices that would improve the effectiveness of their learning. History teaching without the use of the computer will be successful, but children would not gain from the research, simulation and creative work that it makes possible.

However, there is no official place for computer studies in the national curriculum, although it can be taken as an optional subject. Nor is there any promise that microelectronics or even the business use of the technology must be included in certain core or foundation subjects. Complete omission of these topics will be unfortunate, even if they are not taken to the level of examination, for they are all fundamental to being prepared for the society of today, even if we ignore that of tomorrow. Familiarity may come from use across the curriculum, provided that occurs in every subject and the teachers can answer the questions that arise, or even from the use of home computers if the children happen to have them. Clubs can also provide some opportunities for children who choose or are stimulated to join them, particularly for electronics and computing, but as many will not do this, it is hardly the way to promote a well educated population.

If they have no 'official slot' in the curriculum, where can they fit? It is hoped that those responsible for technology will ensure that the rudiments of computer studies and the fundmentals of electronics are taught to all children – both at primary and secondary levels – not as an option but as a central part of the approach to the subject. It may be that in both cases they also find an optional role in later years, but all pupils need an understanding of these basic tools of our society. Those responsible for the science curriculum too should be aware of the important need for all children to know the principles of electronics. Certainly there should be no possibility of any child avoiding a grounding in science and technology. For business studies, if current practice continues, there will be possibilities in the optional subject areas for those destined for a more vocational curriculum. This is only a partial answer, for the practices of commerce and business are a necessary part of the background knowledge of most pupils if any are to join in those areas later in life. Perhaps the only place where they could be introduced is English, where the use of the computer as a wordprocessor can be helpful.

Unfortunately it is clear from the above that the national curriculum, as currently defined, provides a situation in which children will continue to be able to enter and leave school without any grounding in the technology and without having to use it for curricular purposes themselves. To justify this, it may be true that the capital investment in ensuring that a suitable amount of equipment is available is too great for the system at present. While there are shortages of funds, however, the priorities must be questioned. To allow children to leave school to join a society in which the most important tools are based around microprocessors, without learning anything about their fundamental principles or even using them, is surely to misread the aims of education. Experience of the technology is an invaluable introduction to any future life in industry and commerce, and a stimulus to the development of potential small businesses.

Without using the technology, children will miss developing important skills in information handling and being comfortable with the technology. Their opportunities for learning will be restricted and the necessary background for motivating them to learn as adults will be limited. Although there are many statements suggesting feeedom of action for teachers, the drive to testing and a public stance expressed in conventional terms will inhibit them from moving away from the traditional ways of helping children to succeed. In the absence of expectation and some sense of compulsion, only the motivated teachers will ensure an involvement of the technology.

As a scheme, the national curriculum is a preparation for the industrial society. The rigidity of its subject orientation which is timed to fill the learning hours will not encourage the flexibility that is necessary for the information society, nor will the approach underlying pronouncements about the curriculum provide opportunities to develop the confidence and self-knowledge in all children that will be needed. It is not clear that time for the necessary personal and social skill development will be available. Indeed the whole approach within the public statements and the initial signs of implementation is directed towards increasing the accountability and narrowing the options of the industrial curriculum. In the year 2002, when today's four-year-olds leave school, pupils with a different set of skills, knowledge and attitudes will be required for the level of information society they will be joining.

Will there be a new curriculum?

At a time when the national curriculum has just been authorised and its contents are still in the hands of the various panels, it is hard to envisage yet another one appearing. Teachers are still digesting the GCSE, and the national curriculum already poses anxieties, so the thought of a new one on the lines expressed in Part 3 would be very disconcerting. On the other hand, the national curriculum has to turn out to be very different from the ideas that emerged in the various discussions in parliament to provide the basis for the information society. Lord Dainton (1987) said that 'the most damaging possible trend in such a strongly technologically-based society would be a tendency to segregate into two new classes; those who understand and can use the technology and those who do not and who follow instructions', and yet the national curriculum could so easily lead to this.

If changing the curriculum seems difficult, progressing towards new approaches to teaching seems more likely. The extension of the TVEI scheme is not restricted to technology-related subjects but to the whole curriculum, and promises to be primarily about learning processes rather than subject content. One way of approaching this is likely to be funding for a substantial scheme based on supported self-study, making it possible for all local education authorities to experiment with and experience the potential of this system. Teachers will be faced with the task of working as tutors in support of learning in subjects in which they are not expert, and referring children to a range of resources, including other teachers, for any help they may need. Without the technology this will be more difficult, so there are likely to be developments on that front as well.

To be effective, the subjects being learned in this way will be broken into modules, although in the context of the national curriculum these are going to be predominantly mono-disciplinary. However, as some of the best practices of the primary tradition begin to appear in the secondary sector, there will be the opportunity for some cross-disciplinary projects. While these steps will not introduce a full implementation of a curriculum for the information society, some of the essential trends for the approaches to learning may be introduced in a small way.

Little has been mentioned of the value of the technology for those with learning difficulties, whether mental or physical in origin. Many examples of its impact have been recorded in journals, and with further investment it will continue to increase such pupils' opportunities to gain skills as well as helping those with communication problems to attempt a broader curriculum. New technical developments will enhance these options, improving links to computerised devices to make language easier to use in both written and spoken forms. The next stages in technical development will continue the trend to reduce the importance of the keyboard and increase the range of other methods of interacting with microprocessors.

Forecasting the speed and trends of the technology is a dangerous business, for reality usually exceeds imagination. However, it is safe to say that the power and facilities of the equipment will develop at a rapid rate, much in excess of the capability of schools to fund replacements to keep up to date. It will be necessary to skip stages of progress, perhaps introducing a rolling programme of replacement. However, financial planning should be such that no devices are retained for more than five years, not because they are worn out but rather because children should have access to new facilities. Just as nearly all pupils now have calculators, so within a few years all should have their own portable computers that communicate with the school's.

More important, however, are developments in software. Much is expected of expert systems. Children will learn a great deal by analysing particular patterns, for example the optimum conditions for the germination of seeds, devising the rules that apply and inserting them into a system. They may also be useful for teachers in appraising the learning styles of children, and even their common problems. Data handling may also benefit from their application. However, it is very unlikely that they will be used in teaching topics, as the mechanistic approach inherent in the system will run counter to research-based learning.

The important new developments will be in establishing environments into which programs can be imported and used from a wide variety of sources. This does not mean just the simple portability of being able to run a program written for one machine on a different one, but that the software is usable within the operating conditions with which the child is familiar. Such a development will emerge shortly and increase the range of materials that schools will be able to use, including many from other countries.

Technical developments such as these will put further pressure on a curriculum that is locked to subjects and still too concerned with factual content. Accessibility to information and improved communications will provide schools with examples and experiences that will increase the demand for a more open and functional approach to the curriculum, without removing the facility for more academic options.

Pressure will also come from commerce and industry. Their support for a broader approach to A level, as reported by the Higginson Committee (1988), is an indication of an increasing realisation that the industrial curriculum is no longer able to provide an appropriate background for those entering employment. As the changes to the inevitable information society take further shape, pressure from the commercial community will grow. This will be manifested internationally as multinational companies and organisations take a similar attitude.

The importance of the multinational groups will grow as a consquence of the proposed 1992 Single Act that will remove the trade barriers between European Community countries at the end of that year. It is interesting to speculate on the position of the nation state following this and the simultaneous increasing call for more autonomy by communities and regions – a factor that is to be expected as the information society develops. One consequence could well be a growing decentralisation in decision making about the approach to the curriculum.

Changes in other countries will become more widely known and understood by educators as information, experience and materials become more widely disseminated through the communications net-work that the technology is establishing. Together with pressure from commerce and industry, the drive from technological development and the needs within a changing society, the impetus for a curriculum that is more relevant to the information society will grow. The problem is that it takes a great deal of time to develop a curriculum and even longer to prepare the modules for learning. We really cannot afford to delay too much in taking the decision to change.

Will the international community help?

The information society is not a British or even Western phenomenon. It affects all countries, even if the speeds of transition will differ. Each has to face the same problems, aggravated by the increasing mobility of people for work on both long- and short-term bases. No country can continue to act in isolation from others, more especially when many companies have branches in a number of different states and communication systems carry information to the rest of the world. Industry needs similar attitudes and skills from its employees wherever it operates, and it expects a growing compatibility of understanding from its customers wherever they live. At the same time, the nature of the information society will not differ, whatever the country.

Thus, the needs of different countries, have much in common, and a great deal is to be gained from a commonality of purpose within the curriculum of schools. Such a statement raises proper fears for the disappearance of the unique cultural differences between people, but the merit of the open curriculum that was described earlier is that it supports the inclusion of topics that reinforce the bonds within communities. Such a curriculum is designed to ensure that particular cultural characteristics do not die or become fossilised. One of the strengths of humanity is its diversity and the richness of character, tradition and imaginative creativity that results. Any curriculum that does not ensure that this survives and develops destroys some of our inheritance. Through communication systems the variety of cultural traditions will be shared with others and thus enrich the whole, analogous to the maintenance and use of the gene pool that has evolved over time.

The curriculum must relate to the needs of communities, but educators working together at an international level, and with commerce and industry, can also describe the evolving identity of the 'culture générale', the agreed perception of the core skills and insights that should be part of the general wisdom. Such a description would absorb the 'culture technologique', for we are not dealing with two separate cores but one background education for all. A core, like that of an apple, is only a small part of the whole, although there is likely to be considerable commonality about much of the flesh that surrounds it. Decisions on this core are not political but educational - not based on academic esteem but on their utilitarian value within the information society. From them too will develop co-operation in the preparation, production and use of materials for children to use in their learning, and the sharing of information between communities. The problem is that any involvement of governments or their agencies immediately raises barriers and national prejudices, and so this collaborative work will have to be pursued in other ways.

One of the difficulties inhibiting co-operation between nations is the disparity of approaches to learning. The traditions of different societies have encouraged a mixture of habits and attitudes, so that teachers have a diversity of roles. In many countries their status has diminished, particularly where they are seen as information providers and child-minders. Adopting a new curriculum and approaches to learning along the lines described places upon teachers a different emphasis to their role – that of educational consultant. It returns them to the main purpose of their calling – that of helping children to learn. This is a complex position, demanding in its work and requiring a significantly professional attitude. While individual issues may vary, the principal abilities, skills and techniques will be the same in whatever country they are practised, and will also encourage a growing compatibility between the approaches to learning. It is through educational consultants, wherever they work, that the new curriculum will be established and implemented, and advantages for learning taken from the facilities offered by the developing technology.

The implications of the technology for the curriculum are thus an intriguing map of social, political and educational factors. As the information society emerges, brought about by the opportunities provided by the technology, so the demands for a new curriculum will grow, not only in Britain but in every country. The nature of that curriculum and the way it is approached will feed on facilities that the technology has introduced, and children will learn using a variety of microprocessor-based devices. Thus the implications will be at many levels. The options for learning will be opened wider, producing a considerable challenge to the education system to ensure that they can be supported. Adequately resourced, the information society could provide, in the words of Lord Dainton (1987), an 'educational process ... designed to discover and develop latent talents of intellect and personality, and to encourage individuals to be actively autonomous'.

References

Dainton, Lord (1987) *Knowledge is Our Destiny: and Education the Tool* Edward Boyle Memorial Lecture, Royal Society of Arts, 14.1.87

Higginson, G (1988) *Advancing A Levels* HMSO, London

Index